40 Days, 40 Ways is a breath of fresh, joy-filled air and a bountiful resource for the Lenten season. Filled with innovative and thoughtful devotional practices to help you journey closer to Christ, this book offers the potential to turn any forty-day period into a retreat opportunity.

—LISA M. HENDEY, founder of the CatholicMom blog
and author of *The Grace of Yes*

Without exaggeration, I think Marcellino D'Ambrosio is the most readable, understandable, and enjoyable author in religious thought today.

—MOTHER DOLORES HART, Abbey of Regina Laudis

Marcellino D'Ambrosio offers the neophyte as well as the seasoned Catholic a potpourri of Lenten reflections that are as engaging as they are practical. If you want to fall more in love with Jesus, then nourish yourself with *40 Days, 40 Ways!*

—VICTOR GALEONE, Bishop Emeritus of St. Augustine, Florida

In *40 Days, 40 Ways* Marcellino D'Ambrosio has taken me by surprise! He actually has me eager to add to my to-do list and looking forward to forty days of penance. Written in a compelling and engaging style, each daily reflection is packed with quick insight, easy-to-grasp wisdom, and a doable challenge. This book is perfect for even the busiest person seeking to grow closer to God and be created anew.

—KELLY WAHLQUIST, author of *Created to Relate:
God's Design for Peace and Joy*

www.dritaly.com

This book is not just a Lent book, though it is definitely that. Marcellino D'Ambrosio has crafted an approach to faith that rocked my world—part treasury, part practical toolbox, and part kick in the pants!

—SARAH REINHARD, author and blogger

Don't just do something, sit there—especially during Lent. This is the powerful message woven throughout this beautiful devotional from Dr. Italy. *40 Days, 40 Ways* offers spot-on suggestions to help even the busiest of Catholics slow down and spend less time in front of a screen and more time with the Lord. Readers are sure to make this devotional their "go-to" book for Lent—and any time they need to reconnect with Jesus.

—TERESA TOMEO, author and media expert

"This book—like the man who wrote it—is burning with the power of conviction flowing from a two-punch combo of truth and love."

—FR. STAN FORTUNA, C.F.R.

"This is not just another book on Lent. This is book on the magnitude of Christ's love for us during the spiritual season of renewal. Dr. D'Ambrosio challenges us daily to live Lent instead of just waiting it out. But more importantly, Dr. D'Ambrosio helps us open our hearts to Jesus."

—LEAH DARROW

40 Days, 40 Ways

A New Look at Lent

MARCELLINO D'AMBROSIO

servant

AN IMPRINT OF
FRANCISCAN MEDIA
Cincinnati, Ohio

"Behold, I make all things new."
—Revelation 21:5

Cover design by Candle Light Studios
Cover images © Monkey Business Images;
Shutterstock/Lisa F. Young; Shutterstock/Tyler Olson
Book design by Mark Sullivan

LIBRARY OF CONGRESS CATALOGING-IN-PUBLICATION DATA
D'Ambrosio, Marcellino.
40 days, 40 ways : a new look at Lent / Marcellino D›Ambrosio.
pages cm
Includes bibliographical references.
ISBN 978-1-61636-894-4 (alk. paper)
1. Lent. 2. Spiritual life—Catholic Church. I. Title. II. Title: Forty days, forty ways.
BX2170.L4D36 2014
263'.92—dc23
2014033823

ISBN 978-1-61636-894-4

Published by Servant Books, an imprint of
Franciscan Media
28 W. Liberty St.
Cincinnati, OH 45202
www.FranciscanMedia.org

Printed in the United States of America.
Printed on acid-free paper.
15 16 17 18   5 4 3 2

CONTENTS

In the English language, the special season before Easter is called Lent. The word comes from the "lengthening" of daylight hours as we progress from the darkness of winter to the spring sunshine. But other languages, such as Spanish, have a name for this season that is derived from the word for forty. Lent is the season of the forty days.

OK, we do penance for forty days because Jesus fasted forty days in the wilderness. But did you ever wonder why he was out there for forty days rather than seven or ten or fifty?

Think back to the Old Testament. Noah and company were in the ark for forty days. Moses was up on Sinai receiving the Ten Commandments for forty days. The Israelites wandered around the desert for forty years.

Still the question remains: Why forty? Probably because this is the normal number of weeks of human pregnancy.

Each of these biblical "forties" was a necessary yet not-so-comfortable prelude to the birth of something new. In Noah's case, it was the rebirth of a sinful world that had been cleansed by raging floodwaters. In Moses's case, it was the birth of the people of the covenant. For the nomadic Israelites, it was the start of a new, settled existence in the Promised Land.

And Jesus? What did his forty days mean? The birth of a new Israel, liberated from sin, reconciled to God, and governed by the law of the Spirit rather than a law chiseled in stone.

But think back to the story of Moses and the Israelites. Pharaoh did not take the loss of his cheap labor lying down. Likewise, when Jesus begins his mission of liberation, there is another slave master who is no more willing than Pharaoh to let his minions go without a fight.

Our battle is not against flesh and blood, says St. Paul (see Ephesians 6:12). If you don't know your enemy and his strategy, you are bound to lose.

The temptation of Jesus in the desert (Luke 4:1–13) shows us the tactics of this "dark Lord." Bread, a symbol for all that sustains our physical life, is a great blessing. But Satan tries to make material things the ultimate goal, distracting us from a deeper hunger and a more satisfying food. Political leadership is intended by God for the sake of serving the common good; Satan twists things to make leaders self-seeking, oppressive tyrants like himself. Then there is religious temptation, the trickiest of them all—manipulating God for our own glory, using his gifts to make people look at us rather than at him. Sounds a lot like some of the Pharisees.

Jesus triumphs in his forty-day wrestling match. He shows us how to keep from being pinned. Fasting breaks undue attachments to material blessings and stimulates our spiritual appetite. Humble service breaks the stranglehold of pride. The reverent worship of authentic faith releases us from superstition, magic, and all arrogant religion. And the Word of God is revealed as the sword of the Spirit, the secret weapon that slashes through the lies of the enemy.

So our forty days? It should be all about using the tactics modeled by our captain—prayer, fasting, and humble giving—to break all the bonds that hold us back from true spiritual freedom.

We often have a problem, however. Though the season is all about newness, we find ourselves going back to the "same old." "So what are you giving up for Lent?" we often ask each other, as if Lent were mainly a matter of meatless Fridays and forgoing chocolate.

Obviously, if we want to see ourselves emerge from this forty-day challenge as new persons, we will have to go a bit further than this. So in this book, I have collected forty ways to make these forty days a life-changing experience. My aim is to put into your hands a practical manual with new tips, collected from master trainers, to help you burn fat, build spiritual muscle, and win this most critical competition.

The best way to make use of this book is as follows: Set aside fifteen to twenty minutes of quiet time before Lent begins, or as early in Lent as you can. Ask the Holy Spirit, your personal trainer, to guide you. Then prayerfully read through the entire list of forty suggestions provided in the table of contents, looking for just one to three ideas that jump off the page and seem to be, for you, the most important and most doable. Read the specific pages that further explain these particular tips and commit to doing these things faithfully throughout the Lenten season.

Next, commit to read each tip and its accompanying reflection, one per day, from Ash Wednesday all the way to Easter. You will probably find yourself incorporating several more of these spiritual exercises to your regimen as time goes on—if not every day, at least on the day that you read them.

One more thing about the forty days—the Western Christian tradition never counts Sundays as fast days, since they always are a mini-celebration of Christ's resurrection. If you count the days of Lent from Ash Wednesday to Holy Saturday, skipping Sundays, you will count exactly forty "training" days. The six Sundays of Lent are "rest days" when we nonetheless continue to reflect on the great themes of this special season through the Mass readings. We've offered not only training exercises for the forty days, but reflections to nourish you on the rest days as well, not to mention some essays celebrating the victory of Easter. In the appendix at the back of the book, there are specific resources suggested to help you carry out many of the training tips.

If we make good use of this book during this special season of Lent, so pregnant with possibilities, I'm convinced that we will find ourselves breaking through into deeper experience of the joyful liberty and strength that Christ died to win for us. Darkness will give way to increasing light. Something new and wonderful will indeed be born in us!

ACKNOWLEDGMENTS

Writing a book takes lots of preparation. There's proximate preparation—things you do to get ready immediately before you get started. But there's also remote preparation—the groundwork that is often laid months and years before writing begins.

The foundations of this book on the forty days were laid forty years ago when a refugee from hippie culture landed on the doorstep of Our Lady of Providence College Seminary in Warwick, Rhode Island. It was there, under the tutelage of some truly remarkable men, that I discovered the beauty and power of Lent, Holy Week, and the Triduum. To Frs. John Tavares, Robert Hayman, Bob Randall, John Dreher, Enrico Garzilli, and Edward Abbot, I will be eternally grateful.

Many of the essays that make up this book began to take their initial form as articles for several Catholic publications, including *Our Sunday Visitor* and the Catholic News Service syndicated column *Faith Alive*. Here's a shout out to the editors whose requests got the first words flowing: Carole Greene, Rhina Guidos, and Cherie Peacock. And special thanks to Sara Merlene Kluth, who has spent countless late nights since 2003 sharing many of these essays with the world as blog posts on the Crossroads Initiative website (dritaly.com).

Finally, besides my family and the Crossroads board, benefactors, volunteers, and office staff who make my ministry possible, I want to thank Claudia Volkman and Louise Paré for putting me up to writing this book; Katie Carroll, my valiant and cheerful editor, and all the folks at Franciscan Media who are so determined to make a book like this available in all platforms, including audio: Sharon Cross, Matt Wielgos, Judy Zarick, and Ron Riegler.

DAY 1

Ashes are a sign of humbling oneself before God. Receive them and pray for humility.

Lent means repentance. And one definition of repentance is to humble oneself before the Lord. While we forgo the sackcloth of the Old Testament, we still begin the Lenten season with ashes on our forehead, a sign of humility.

But we need to stop here and correct a common misconception. Lots of people think that humility means being down on yourself. Shrinking from a challenge. Being shy, retiring, soft-spoken.

In the Catholic tradition, it means nothing of the sort. We believe that men and women are destined for greatness. Being created in the image of God means that we have incomparable dignity. Even the ancient philosophers, without the benefit of revelation, knew that we human beings have an irrepressible desire to accomplish great deeds and "become someone." St. Thomas Aquinas and the entire Catholic tradition agree that the desire for excellence and achievement is natural and good, not sinful and proud.

So it was not wrong for James and John (Mark 10:35) to ask to sit at Jesus's right and left (in Matthew 20:20, it is their Jewish mother who does the lobbying). The problem is, they are clueless about what sitting at Jesus's right and left means. So Jesus tells them.

It means serving. Till it hurts. Even unto death.

Most would agree that you can't get any higher or greater than God. But what Jesus comes to reveal to us is a God who is a community of love, three persons whose ceaseless activity, whose joy, consists in giving themselves, each to the other, in love, for all eternity. When the human race is taken captive by sin, the second person of this Holy Trinity empties himself of divine glory and unites himself forever to a human nature in the womb of a virgin. The greatness of divine love means that the omnipotent one now allows himself to become helpless, the infinite one now becomes small, the one who has no needs now becomes vulnerable. In his thirty-three years he does many great deeds—healing the incurable, driving out demons, even raising the dead. But his greatest deed was to offer himself as a ransom, so that all humanity could be released from its bondage (Isaiah 53:11).

Divine love, agape, charity. It is in this that true greatness lies. When divine love encounters human need and suffering, it will stop at nothing to meet that need and relieve that suffering. Even if it means washing feet, or changing a soiled diaper (a contemporary equivalent of foot-washing), or dying on a cross.

So attaining greatness for us means not to claw our way to the top, stepping on whomever gets in our way. This is pride and is a sign not of strength, but of weakness. Among the Gentiles, "their great ones make their importance felt" (see Mark 10:42) because it comforts them to get acclaim, however insincere, from the masses. It at least temporarily drowns out the inner voice of self-doubt and insecurity that is the hidden motivation of the bully and the dictator.

Humility is possible only for the free. Those who are secure, as Jesus was, in the Father's love, have no need of pomp and circumstance or people fawning on them. They know who they are, where they've come from, and where they are going. Not taking themselves too seriously, they can laugh at themselves. The proud cannot. Notice the similarity between the words *humility* and *humor* (and *human*, for that matter).

Humility means having a true estimate of oneself. Being human means that I'm made in God's image and likeness. Therefore I'm gifted; I have dignity and a great destiny. But being human also means that I'm a creature, not the Creator. I have limits that I need to recognize and respect. "Remember, man, that thou art dust and unto dust thou shalt return." Note how the word *humility* also resembles the word *humus*, that component of soil that makes it fertile.

St. Paul talks about the Christian life as a race, and encourages us to run so as to win (1 Corinthians 9:24ff). So it's not just OK, it's commanded to be competitive, to strive to excel. But true greatness consists in sharing in the sacrificial love of Christ, who comes to serve rather than to be served. That means that this race St. Paul is talking about is a race to the bottom.

DAY 2

Examine your media consumption—news, music, TV, sports, and social media.
Decide how you can cut back to reduce the noise and open up time for prayer,
service, and personal relationship with others. If you have drive time, listen
to Catholic radio, talks, or audiobooks instead of news, sports, and music (see
suggestions in the Lenten Resources, on page 116).

George Gallup once conducted a poll called "Religion in America." He studied two groups of Americans: regular churchgoers from various Christian churches on the one hand, and totally unchurched people on the other. He quizzed both groups on issues ranging from the divinity of Jesus, to cheating on income tax, infidelity in marriage, and abortion.

His findings were shocking. Fully 88 percent of the churchgoers had answers identical to those of the unchurched people. Only 12 percent of the churchgoers had opinions and lifestyles that were recognizably Christian.

Hold it! Ephesians 4:17–24 tells us that to be a Christian means to live in a radically different way than the pattern offered by the pagan society that surrounds us. Being a Christian means acquiring a new mind and becoming a new person who reflects the image and likeness of a holy God.

So why don't 88 percent of churchgoers get it? They have presumably heard this passage in Church more than once.

Maybe it is because the adage is true—you are what you eat.

Recently I heard someone quip that if you are what you eat, most Americans are fast, easy, and cheap. But scarier than what we put into our mouths is what we put into our minds. The average American watches about twenty hours of TV per week. When not watching the tube, we are often online, scanning a magazine, or listening to our iPods. Should we be surprised that our values generally reflect the values of the entertainment industry and news media? After all, you are what you eat.

That's why Jesus offers himself to us as the bread of life, the bread that comes down from heaven. Since the sixteenth century, people have often debated the meaning of John 6. Should we interpret the manna from heaven to be his Word—or rather, the Eucharist? The Mass shows us that it need not be either/or. An ancient tradition dating back to the early Church Fathers says that we feed on Christ from two tables, the table of the Word, symbolized by the ambo, and the table of the Eucharist, which is the altar.

Each Mass offers a feast of God's Word not only in the readings but in the prayers and acclamations which are often direct quotes or paraphrases from Scripture. The Word of God in the liturgy is like a double-edged sword (see Hebrews 4:12) that penetrates deep, challenging us, healing our wounds, enlightening our minds, directing our steps. It stimulates the eyes of faith to recognize the Body and Blood of Christ under the humble signs of bread and wine. The Eucharist is indeed the most substantial food he offers us. We are called to be the Body of Christ. Why did he give us his Body, Blood, Soul, and Divinity under the forms of bread and wine? Because you are what you eat.

Lots of Catholics who regularly come to Mass are part of the 88 percent nominal majority. Why is that? Because the Word and the Eucharist can only be eaten by faith and digested by those who are not bloated with junk food. Many scarcely hear the Sunday readings because their minds are filled with the song they were listening to on the way to Church or the items on their to-do list. Many hear but quickly forget since they don't feed on God's Word again until the next time they are at Sunday Mass.

If we carefully examined the 12 percent of churchgoers with a recognizably Christian lifestyle, I bet we'd find that most of them shy away from intellectual junk food, coming to Mass hungry (maybe that's the point of the hour-long pre-Communion fast). I bet they provide some time to digest the Word and the Eucharist through regular moments of quiet prayer throughout the week. And I bet they are smart enough to know that you don't eat just once a week and expect to run the race to win (see 1 Corinthians 9:24). Like the Israelites in the desert, these Christians gather the manna of God's Word every day and make it their daily bread. Some even attend the Eucharist daily.

Besides their lives being more inspiring, the lives of the 12 percent in Gallup's poll exhibited one further characteristic. They were considerably happier than both the unchurched and the nominal Christians who were equally plagued with a vague sense of emptiness.

Junk food may taste good, but it often leaves you with indigestion. But the Bread of Life satisfies. We were made for it. As Jesus says, "No one who comes to me shall ever be hungry, no one who believes in me shall thirst again" (see John 6:35).

Plan to get to confession at least once during Lent after making an extensive examination of conscience.

As I crossed the great divide of puberty, I formed a vivid image of God. He was a grumpy old man on a throne with a frown on his face. Every time anyone tried to have a little fun, he'd shout, "Thou shalt not!"

To really live and not just exist, you had to do the daring, "sinful" things. What the Bible calls "sin" is where the action is, it seemed.

This is what I believed because this is what I was taught in the movies I watched and the books I read. It's what I heard in the locker room and in the checkout line, from men and women, young and old. Everybody appeared to accept this as a matter of fact.

Behind this widespread perception is a very successful propaganda campaign unparalleled in the history of humanity. In fact it goes back to the very beginnings of humanity—all the way back to the Garden of Eden (see Genesis 3).

Think of it for a minute. The triune God, completely sufficient in himself and needing nothing, decides to create paradise out of chaos in an act of sheer generosity. He creates creatures of all shapes and sizes, and appoints as caretakers of them all a pair who is created in God's own image and likeness, with intellect and will, freedom and responsibility. Their assigned activity is to love one another intimately, to walk daily with God in the cool of the evening, and simply enjoy paradise. Any duties? Sort of. They had to tend the garden, which was maintenance-free given the fact that neither thorn nor thistle, neither drought nor Japanese beetle had as yet arrived on the scene. And there was one more responsibility: to avoid eating the fruit of a particular tree, since it would kill them. But how hard was that, given all the other luscious fruit available in the garden?

Then appears a slithering reptile who had given them nothing of what they enjoyed. But now he has the nerve to give them advice.

"Did God say you'd die if you ate this fruit? Nonsense! He only said that because eating this fruit would make you his equal, and he can't bear that. You see, he created you to enslave you. He wants to keep you under his foot. He's keeping the best for himself. You listen to him and you'll be missing out on real life. You'll never be free."

Thus began the deceptive advertising campaign that lasts till this day, the glamorization of death. For that truly is what sin is about, and that's why God says, "Thou shalt not." He is not a crabby prude, but a loving Father. He knows us better than we know ourselves and loves us more than we love ourselves. So he does what every parent does. "Don't touch the stove; you'll get burnt." "Don't play at the top of the stairs; you'll fall and break your neck."

Our first parents believed the liar instead of the Father. They fell and broke their relationship with God and shattered the innocent intimacy they had with one another. As soon as it started, their family fragmented with Cain killing Abel. Thorns and thistles appeared, paradise was lost, and death came into the world.

Lent begins with the memory of how the first head of the human family buckled under the pressure of the lies. But more importantly, we remember how the New Adam (see Romans 5) went another round with the deceiver and vanquished him through the power of the Word of God (see Matthew 4:1–11).

Our task during these forty days is to examine our lives in light of God's Word and see where we've allowed darkness to creep in, where we've taken the bait of the diabolical fisher of men. It's time to use the sword of the Spirit to cut through his web of deception, to free ourselves from the net that holds us as prey.

That is why Lent is called a joyful season of freedom. The purple color of repentance is also the color of royalty—it's the time to recognize our true identity and claim our true birthright as free sons and daughters of a loving Father who happens to be the King of the Universe.

DAY 4

Examine your consumption patterns. Is there anything you can sacrifice for a while? Starbucks? A few beers? Restaurant meals or movies? Cut back and give the saved money to those in need.

Everyone knows that Lent is about sacrifice. So it's only fitting at the beginning of Lent to recall one of the most famous sacrifices of all time.

Here's the background. Abraham really only desires one thing: a son who will lead to descendants as numerous as the stars of the sky. The only problem is that his wife is barren and advanced in years. So he tries to solve the problem in his own way, and produces a son by a slave girl. This doesn't work out very well, and both the slave and her son are sent away. Next God intervenes, works a miracle, and causes the elderly Sarah to conceive and bear a son. Isaac, then, is not only the legitimate firstborn son of Abraham but his last hope. There is absolutely nothing more precious to Abraham than Isaac. Indeed, to give up his son would be to give up himself.

This, by the way, is the true meaning of sacrifice in the ancient world. God deserves everything because he has given us everything. So ancient peoples instinctively knew that authentic sacrifice could never be just a nod to God. Rather, it had to be big and precious enough to represent their entire lives. That's why human sacrifice was so prevalent in ancient times—the offering of the firstborn was seen as the only adequate worship of the gods responsible for our very existence. In Genesis 22, God stops Abraham before he slays his son. The ordeal was just a test to see if Abraham was truly devoted to God in faith, obedience, and gratitude. God does not want Isaac's blood…only Abraham's heart. So he provides a substitute, a ram, which shows the true meaning of all authentic sacrifice—we give to God something precious that represents our very selves.

But the image of Isaac carrying the wood for the sacrifice up the slope of Mt. Moriah should tip us off that this story points beyond itself to a future sacrifice beyond all comprehension. The ram caught in the thicket is not the true substitute, and the true sacrifice does not take place upon Moriah. It is the Lamb, not the ram, God's Son, not Abraham's, that is offered. Like Isaac, he carried the wood of the sacrifice up the slope of Mt. Calvary. But unlike Isaac, he did so freely, knowing what that sacrifice would cost him. And his sacrifice accomplishes what no animal sacrifice possibly could—the eternal salvation of all who are willing to accept this free gift of love.

This is what the whole story is about. From Genesis to Revelation, the theme is the astonishing love of God. The love of the Father for his Incarnate Word: "This is my Son, my Beloved" (Mark 9:7). The love of the Father who sacrifices that beloved Son for us (see John 3:16). The love of the Son who leaves behind the brilliant cloud of Mt. Tabor for the agony of Calvary.

Though it is we who owe everything to God, it is he who sacrifices everything for us. Our love for him can only be a faint echo of his unstoppable love for us. "Is it possible that he who did not spare his own Son but handed him over for the sake of us all will not grant us all things besides?" (see Romans 8:32).

So this is the true meaning of Lenten sacrifice. We renew and deepen our dedication to him and express that by sacrificing something meaningful to us. But as we go about our fasting and almsgiving, let's not forget to give him some extra time in prayer. After all, on the Mount of Transfiguration (see Matthew 17:5), God did not ask us to give up chocolate. But, after identifying Jesus as his beloved Son, he did give us a very clear command. He said, "Listen to him!"

The Temptation of Christ

In today's fuzzy moral landscape, it is quite unpopular to even speak of sin, never mind condemn it. It's even more politically incorrect to talk about God taking stern action against sin and those who promote it.

But that is exactly what the story of Noah is all about (see Genesis 9:8–15). The great flood is a testament to God's hatred of sin and determination to wipe it from the face of the earth. He, of course, offers a way to escape the waters of destruction. He instructs Noah to build an ark, which carries to safety eight people and a pair of every animal. With these, he provides the earth and the human race with a new beginning. As a sign of God's covenant of friendship with the newly recreated world, he places a rainbow in the sky.

From the beginning, Christians have seen in this story a hint of a greater work of God that would come later. The first flood swept away the evil from the surface of the earth, but not from the hearts of the ark's passengers. The Red Sea closing in upon Pharaoh and his armies had much the same limitation—it did not cleanse the soul of Israel.

Therefore an even greater act of salvation was needed, one that was more radical, that penetrated to the very root of evil. God himself enters into our world in the form of a man and engages in hand-to-hand combat with the father of lies. First Jesus himself is immersed in the waters, a sign of the destruction of sin, though he himself has no sin. Next he goes into the wilderness to strike at sin's agent.

The wrestling match is won by the Son. This, however, is not the decisive battle. Mark is a Gospel writer of few words (see Mark 1:12–15) and does not relate what Luke tells us: Satan left Jesus to await another opportunity (see Luke 4:13). That opportunity came later, brokered by Judas, Caiaphas, and Pilate. By means of the cross, the sign of this New Covenant, Jesus decisively vanquished sin and its patron, letting loose from his pierced side a stream that was more powerful than the ancient waters traversed by Noah and Moses. Through faith and immersion in these mighty waters of baptism, sin can finally be scoured not just from the skin but from the heart, putting to death not men, but the old humanity, separated from God and infected with the disease of disobedience. In 1 Peter 3:20 we see something we might easily miss: There happened to be eight persons in the ark. Jesus rose from the dead the day after the Sabbath, the "eighth day." God created the old world in six days, rested on the seventh, and performed the new creation on the eighth. For this reason, in the early Church, baptisms did not usually take place inside the main church sanctuary. Rather, smaller buildings called baptisteries were erected next door to the church. It is notable that they were generally octagonal—eight-sided. Why? Because baptism means burying the old man with Christ and emerging from the womb of the Church as a new creation, sharing in Christ's resurrection.

Lent is a time intimately linked with baptism. In the early Church, it was the season when catechumens prepared themselves through prayer and fasting for their paschal journey to the baptistery. The faithful prayed and fasted with them. It was also the time when those who had soiled the white garments of their baptism through sin prepared for reconciliation during the sacred Triduum.

If we're honest, all of us fall to some degree into that second category. So let us determine—through prayer, fasting, and giving—to intercede for the catechumens and candidates and, at the same time, to scour lukewarmness and compromise from our own hearts. Procrastination and excuses must be put to death. Now is the acceptable time; now is the day of salvation!

DAY 5

Commit to a daily time of quiet prayer. Don't do all the talking: Make sure at least part of this time is spent listening to God through Scripture and silence.

A lady once wrote me a harsh letter protesting that she could find the word *Catholic* nowhere in the Bible.

True, the earliest occurrence of the term is in a letter of St. Ignatius of Antioch, written about twenty years after the New Testament. But the idea that the Church is "catholic" pops up everywhere in the Gospels and epistles. The Greek word *catholic* comes from the word meaning "wholeness" or "fullness." The "catholic" church is not just a regional sect for an exclusive little group. Rather it must include the *whole* family of God over the *whole* world, welcoming *all*, from every tribe, tongue, people, and nation (see Revelation 7:9). In addition, the "catholic" church cannot pick and choose which doctrines are trendy and convenient but must be faithful to the *whole* truth. Paul points out that the essence of his apostolic call was to be a "catholic" teacher: "I became a minister of this church through the commission God gave me to preach among you his word in its fullness…. We admonish all men and teach them in the full measure of wisdom, hoping to make every man complete in Christ" (Colossians 1:25, 28, *NAB*).

One day, the fullness of life and truth came walking into the living room of a pair of sisters named Martha and Mary (see Luke 10:38–42). They immediately recognized the privilege of having Jesus in their home and set to work fulfilling the sacred duty of hospitality.

The problem was, they had conflicting ideas of what that duty entailed. Martha's response is very recognizable, especially by those raised in Mediterranean culture. "Bring out the coffee, the wine (what kind do you prefer?), make sure the china and silverware are laid out in proper order, get out a full assortment of hot and cold hors d'oeurves (make sure the hot are really served hot!)."

Mary thought that the supreme compliment that she could pay to her divine guest, even more than world-class refreshments, was to give him her full attention. The fullness of truth had come to her home to nourish, enlighten, and transform her. Not to receive and unwrap this wonderful gift would be an insult to the giver.

Martha's mistake was not that she attended to the guest's bodily needs. The story of Martha and Mary is not an endorsement of laziness and passivity. In Genesis 18:1–10, God visits Abraham in the form of three travelers, and Abraham and Sarah pull out all the stops when it comes to food and drink, and this was good.

Martha's problem was that she allowed the *action* of hospitality to become a *distraction*. She couldn't see the forest for the trees. She lost her focus and actually got mad that her sister would not join her in her frenetic fussing.

Mary maintained her focus. She was not passive—attentiveness to the fullness of truth is supremely active. That's why the contemplative, monastic life has always been held in the highest esteem in the Catholic Church.

A monk once told me that the greatest sin of the modern world is not its lewdness but its busyness. We live in the most distracted, frenetic society of all time. It is tempting in such a society to think we are good Catholics because God is part of our life and to feel that we deserve applause because we look at him from time to time out of the corner of our eye.

The fullness of truth, the fullness of life, the fullness of grace deserves our full attention. Jesus really cannot be merely a part of our life; he must be the center of our life. This doesn't mean that our life can't be full of activities. But unless we preserve some quiet time each day to sit at his feet as did Mary, our action will become distraction, and we'll be as snappy and unhappy as Martha.

DAY 6

Spend the first available ten minutes of the day thanking God for everything you are grateful for...before you ask for anything! This can even be done in the car as you are driving to work or school.

A few months before he died, St. John Paul II surprised the world with his announcement of a special Year of the Eucharist. Why a whole year? Because the Eucharist, in the words of St. Thomas Aquinas, is the sacrament of sacraments. In all the sacraments, Christ gives to us the transforming power of his love, which we call "grace." But in the Eucharist, and only in the Eucharist, Jesus gives us even more. He gives us his entire self—Body and Blood, Soul and Divinity.

Of course, the proper response to a gift of this magnitude is gratitude. Offering thanksgiving to God first and foremost is a strict obligation of justice. We were created out of nothing, through no effort of our own. We were saved by grace; it was not our own doing (see Ephesians 2:4-5). On both counts, we owe God everything. We can never adequately repay him, and so we owe him a lifetime of gratitude. That's why Abraham Lincoln proclaimed an annual holiday of Thanksgiving in America. That's why we Catholics speak of our "Sunday obligation." We are bound, if we are able, to observe the third commandment and keep the Lord's Day holy by gathering together to give thanks. *Eucharist*, by the way, means "thanksgiving." In the ancient dialogue between priest and people that introduces the Eucharistic (thanksgiving) Prayer, we say that to give him thanks is "right and just."

Why must we discharge this obligation at Mass rather than in the comfort of our own homes? Because our sacrifice of thanksgiving is weak and insufficient on its own. Only One offered a perfect sacrifice of praise to the Father, and that sacrifice is made present again at every Eucharist. Our inadequate "thanks" is absorbed into the perfect sacrifice of the Son much like the drop of insipid water is absorbed into the rich wine that becomes Christ's blood.

But thanksgiving can't be limited to Sunday Eucharist. We are called to develop a lifestyle of thanksgiving and become a Eucharistic people. St. John Paul II, in his letter announcing the Year of the Eucharist, directed us to develop a Eucharistic attitude that extends beyond the Mass into every area of life. It means recognizing that though he is most fully present in the Blessed Sacrament, the Lord is really present and active everywhere, providing for us, loving us, and challenging us to grow. It means remembering what the secularized Western world has forgotten, that all is an undeserved gift from a transcendent creator.

So before we eat, we pause to say thanks, recognizing that all material blessings are gifts from a loving Father. We decide to spend a greater percentage of our prayer time giving thanks for received blessings than asking him for new ones. We learn to thank him even in trials and tragedies—even for trials and tragedies (1 Thessalonians 5:16; James 1:2), knowing that he is powerful enough to bring greater good from them, as he did from the horror of the cross.

A Eucharistic attitude means bringing the Eucharist into daily life, but it also means bringing our daily lives into the Eucharist. During the Eucharistic Prayer, I silently add in thanks for my personal blessings of home and work, of food on the table, and the health of my family. I also thank God for my own salvation history, especially for plucking me out of dangerous teenage waters. I thank God for bringing me together with a woman who loves him and loves me, and for having kept us faithful for many years. I thank him for our own family's salvation history.

There's a funny thing about gratitude. It keeps us focused on our blessings, which fills us with joy and a childlike sense of wonder. A Eucharistic attitude, then, is a key to the abundant life (see John 10:10) and the fullness of joy (see John 15:11) that Jesus came to bring us.

DAY 7

The official prayer book of the Catholic Church is the book of Psalms. Pray at least one psalm per day. Once you get that down, increase it to two, three, or more. The best way to do this is by praying the Liturgy of the Hours, which can be followed very easily online at universalis.com or through smartphone apps such as Laudate and iBreviary.

I've often heard people say that they don't want to trouble God with their petty needs and concerns. After all, he has more important things to attend to, like running the universe.

Yet the New Testament makes God out to be a glutton for punishment. Not only does Jesus often urge us to ask for what we need—"Ask and you shall receive" (see Luke 11:9), but he praises those, like Bartimaeus, who ask in the loudest, most obnoxious of ways (see Mark 10:46–52). To top it off, he tells stories that showcase rude, relentless people who wake up their neighbors in the middle of the night (see Luke 11:5–8). My all-time favorite is the story of the nagging widow who won't give the judge a moment's rest until she gets what she wants (Luke 18:1–8).

The unjust judge simply wanted to get the lady off his back. He wanted the widow to stop bugging him. But God appears to want us to bug him. And keep bugging him. Why? Maybe because he'd rather we look to him for assistance than to the idols of this age. Perhaps because he knows that asking for help strengthens the virtue of humility in us since it is an admission that we are not in total control of the universe and just might need him. Perhaps because he is a loving Father and likes being with us, even when we come just to ask him to open his wallet.

When I was a teen, I thought that prayer was about asking for stuff. I prayed that God would keep my parents from finding out about certain things I'd done. I prayed that the best-looking girl in the class would like me. After all, Scripture says to ask.

But Scripture also tells us what to ask for. And there is the rub. We are often wrong about what to ask for, because we misidentify what will really make us happy. God knows us better than we know ourselves, since he created us. And he loves us more than we love ourselves, because he is our Father.

So before talking to him, which is certainly one dimension of prayer, we need to listen to him, which is an even more important dimension of prayer. We were given two ears and only one mouth for a reason.

But how do we listen to him? One privileged way is through Scripture. These words are guaranteed to be his, for they are inspired, breathed by the Holy Spirit, divine words in human words (see 2 Timothy 3:16). This does not just mean that the Holy Spirit moved once, guiding the authors at the moment they wrote down the words thousands of years ago. It means the Holy Spirit dwells in these words as in a temple and beckons us to enter to meet him regularly for a life-changing rendezvous. These words are not simply a wearying catalogue of ideas we need to buy into, facts we need to believe, or rules we need to observe. Instead they are meant to be a fresh, personal, energizing communication from God each time we hear or read them. They are food for our souls.

Most of us don't eat once a week. We eat daily. Several times a day, in fact. So we should gather up the manna of God's word at least daily, maybe even several times a day.

So you don't have much time for quiet prayer and extensive Bible reading? Join the club. You may not have time for a daily Thanksgiving feast, but I bet you snack a few times a day. There are scriptural, bite-sized snacks called the psalms that have been the backbone of prayer for God's people for nearly three thousand years. The psalms are God's inspired word through which he speaks to us, but they happen to be cast as prayers that we can speak to him. That kills two birds with one stone. And they cover everything that we could possibly want to say to God. "Thank you," "Praise you," "Why are you doing this to me?" "Please help me," and so on. There are even a few asking God to smash our enemies. These would have been perfect for Moses to have used while praying during the battle with Amalek (see Exodus 17:8–13), except they hadn't been written yet.

If you have time for three meals or snacks a day, you have time for at least three psalms a day.

DAY 8

Stimulate your spiritual appetite. Find a form of fasting appropriate for you, given your age, state of health, and state in life. Some fast on bread and water on Wednesdays and Fridays. Some fast from sweets or alcohol throughout Lent. Some fast one or more days per week from breakfast all the way to dinner, spending the lunch hour in prayer or at noon Mass.

Jesus's Sermon on the Mount is probably the most famous sermon of all time. And the opening lines of that sermon are equally famous. For two thousand years they've been known as "the Beatitudes" (see Matthew 5:1–12).

In nine short verses, Jesus lays out the character sketch of the spiritually successful person who is truly blest, fortunate, and positioned to experience perfect happiness and the fullness of joy. This is what *beatitude* means.

Now the very first qualification takes us back a bit. "Blessed are the poor in spirit." Is Jesus endorsing indigence? Is he a Marxist who champions the proletariat and vilifies the bourgeoisie?

Not at all. Note that he is talking about the "poor in spirit" here—in other words, those who are aware of their own emptiness. The poor in spirit are not those who beat themselves up, but those who frankly recognize how puny they are before the mysteries of the universe and the creator of that universe. They don't let their own accomplishments and abilities blind them to their mortality and vulnerability. They don't fool themselves.

Jesus mentions elsewhere how hard it is for the rich to enter the kingdom because it is very easy for the successful to lose touch with their neediness and actually believe the flattery of their fan club. Those who are not influential, educated, or wealthy have an easier time recognizing their need since it stares them in the face every place they turn. For this reason, such people streamed into the Church during the New Testament era (see 1 Corinthians 1:26–31) as they do today.

The poor in spirit are empty and long to be filled. They hunger and thirst for the wholeness that is called holiness, for the food that truly satisfies.

The rich in spirit don't hunger for anything. They are self-satisfied and "full of themselves." When offered an opportunity to grow spiritually, they protest: "But I'm a good person and worship God in my own way," or, "I go to Mass every Sunday; isn't that enough?" They are too busy for prayer and yawn when exposed to a spiritual discussion. They are too absorbed with themselves to be interested in God. They may be able to get excited about the World Cup, but never about heaven.

This lack of spiritual hunger, this utter apathy in the face of the things of God, is actually one of the seven deadly sins. It is called *sloth,* or spiritual laziness, and it is one of the most striking characteristics of contemporary western society. Sloth is a sneaky sin that quietly creeps into the lives of people, even religious ones, and gradually chokes out true spirituality. It diverts our attention from the things of heaven to a myriad of other things until we find ourselves bored with God, making only routine and mechanical efforts to "fulfill our Sunday obligation." There is no passion, no zeal, no desire. Just lots of excuses.

"Blessed are the single-hearted, for they shall see God." The hearts of the blessed, the truly happy, are not divided between God and football and career and money. Those who are truly happy have only one God, and they look to him alone to be filled. If they play sports, they do it for his honor and glory, not theirs. If they marry, they love Christ and are loved by Christ through their spouse. If they pursue a career or build a business, they do it according to his will to advance his kingdom.

Reading the Sermon on the Mount, and especially the Beatitudes, is a gut check for us all. It's one of the best examinations of conscience around, perfect to read before every confession and every Lent. Incidentally, that's what the penitential season of Lent is about. Fasting is meant to restimulate our spiritual appetite. Spiritual exercises are designed to shrug off the laziness of sloth. Christianity is not just a matter of believing in God, but avidly pursuing him.

DAY 9

Get to daily Mass. If you can't get to Mass daily, try at least to go on Fridays as well as Sunday in gratitude for Christ's sacrifice. Maybe you can go another day or two per week as well.

Have you ever felt unappreciated? Imagine how Elijah felt in 1 Kings 19. He had just brought an end to drought and famine through his intercession, had rid the land of a host of false prophets, and had run something like thirty miles in the rain to bring the good news to the capital city. And what thanks did he get? Queen Jezebel vowed to take his life. So now, rather than being honored as a hero, he found himself fleeing for his life into the desert. Discouragement, despair, and self-pity are understandable in these circumstances.

Yet Elijah points to another whose kindness is met with even more shocking ingratitude. Jesus healed, fed, and raised from the dead many more than Elijah. He preached to multitudes of weary, downtrodden people who were enlivened by his words. Where were these on Good Friday morning when the crowd was given a choice between Jesus and Barabbas?

In Jesus's mouth we find no words of self-pity. He prays instead that his captors be forgiven, "for they know not what they do." The words that some interpret as despairing, "My God, My God, why hast thou forsaken me," are really a prophetic utterance indicating that Psalm 22, where these words are found, is being fulfilled in what is happening to him.

Jesus did not undertake his mission to please the crowds or to bask in the waves of their adulation. He had no illusions about us and no need of our gratitude. After all, he is God. What then was he doing it all for? The rigors of his public ministry, the horror of his suffering and criminal's death—how do we interpret it? St. Paul tells us: "He gave himself for us as an offering to God, a gift of pleasing fragrance" (Ephesians 5:2).

It was a gift—for us, for the Father. He walked in what Ephesians calls the way of love. Agape or charity, the kind of love we are dealing with here, is precisely this—the pure gift of self.

But we are not God. How can we love this way when even the prophet Elijah wrestled with despair and self-pity in the face of rejection? The answer for us is the same as the answer for him. God provided supernatural food which gave Elijah the energy to go on, to keep walking through the dry, blistering heat all the way from southern Israel to the Sinai desert, forty days' worth of desert journey. The food he was given must have been some powerful nourishment indeed!

We are dealing here with what the Church Fathers, following St. Paul, called a "type," a prefigurement of a New Testament reality. In John 6 we learn that this new food is Jesus's very Body and Blood offered to us under the signs of bread and wine. Jesus tells us that the manna given the Israelites to sustain them in their desert journey is another "type" of this new, supernatural nourishment.

In the sacrament of the altar, Jesus holds nothing back from us. He gives us his whole self, his humanity and his divinity, including that mysterious divine love of the Trinity, *agape*—the self-giving love that empowers Jesus and the saints to love without counting the cost, to love to the end.

To love in this way, for us human beings, is not natural. It is supernatural. To do it we need supernatural food, food that causes the eternal life of God to course through our veins. This, in fact, is what the Eucharist is—heavenly food for the desert journey.

There certainly are moments of joy this side of heaven. But the way of the Christian always involves the way of the cross. At some point, like Elijah, we must pass through the dark valley of misunderstanding and the desert of ingratitude. It is only through an intimate union with Christ, deepened and nourished by the sacrament of his body and blood, that we'll have the power to complete that journey and to do so with a smile instead of a scowl.

DAY 10

Learn the corporal and spiritual works of mercy. Identify one to begin incorporating into your life this Lent.

The Seven Corporal Works of Mercy: to feed the hungry, give drink to the thirsty, clothe the naked, shelter the homeless, visit the sick, ransom captives, and bury the dead.

The Seven Spiritual Works of Mercy: to instruct the ignorant, counsel the doubtful, admonish sinners, bear wrongs patiently, forgive others willingly, comfort the afflicted, and pray for the living and the dead.

The Eucharist is the "source and summit" of the Christian life. That does not mean that it is the sum total of the Christian life.

Indeed, the Eucharist and all the sacraments are memorials of a dramatic act of mercy that took place not in the serene majesty of the temple liturgy, but in history, amidst the hustle and bustle of everyday life.

Let's pause for a moment to recall the reason for this Ultimate Work of Mercy. The first members of the human race had renounced their freedom and dignity as sons and daughters of God and had fallen into bondage to a tyrannical master. Suffering and death were the fruit of this slavery. The price to redeem themselves from this miserable situation was beyond their means. So in bondage they stayed, forging heavier chains for themselves with every passing generation.

Until, that is, the God of Justice manifested himself as the Father of Mercy. Justice renders to each of us our due and calls us to assume responsibility for ourselves. Mercy goes beyond the issues of who is responsible. Mercy is simply love's response to suffering. So the Father of Mercy, to relieve our suffering, sent his Eternal Son to be made flesh by the power of the Holy Spirit. God the Son, by nature incapable of suffering, became vulnerable for us. He bound the strong man who had tyrannized the human race and paid the debt that the human race hadn't been able to cover. His rescue mission succeeded at the cost of his life.

This is what the Mass commemorates and makes present again. He who once gave himself in mercy to relieve our suffering continues to give himself to us, holding nothing back, in the sacrament of sacraments, the sacrament of divine mercy.

But why does he give himself under the form of food? That we may become what we eat. That we may grow in holiness, which is to say, become more perfect in that divine love that we call charity. Mercy is just what charity becomes when it encounters suffering.

The Eucharist, then, cannot exist in isolation from life. It is the liturgical commemoration of a Work of Mercy that is designed to issue forth in works of mercy. Thus mercy is essential to the life of every member of the Church until evil and suffering are no more. St. James reminds us that a Christianity that responds to suffering with no more than kind words and tender sentiments is neither true love nor even authentic faith: "If a brother or sister is ill-clad and in lack of daily food, and one of you says to them, 'Go in peace, be warmed and filled,' without giving them the things needed for the body, what does it profit?" (James 2:14–17)

Some things to keep in mind about the works of mercy in the Church:

1. Mercy is for everyone. One of the greatest misconceptions of my early years was that Catholicism is a two-track system. Laypeople just need to worry about keeping the precepts of the Church and the Ten Commandments. The Sermon on the Mount and true holiness are the territory of those called to priesthood and religious life. Knowing that this misconception was pervasive, the Second Vatican Council affirmed in its Dogmatic Constitution on the Church that the call to holiness is absolutely universal (see *Lumen Gentium,* 5). And holiness means love, and love means mercy. Therefore, works of mercy can't be relegated only to those who belong to the social justice committee or the Missionaries of Charity. Everyone, without exception, is called to the works of mercy.

2. Mercy relieves suffering, and there are different kinds of suffering. I once heard someone offer a striking petition during the Prayer of the Faithful: "Let us pray for all those suffering from the pain of not knowing the love of

God." The lack of bodily necessities certainly causes great distress. But so does the lack of the things of the spirit. It is important to keep in mind that the Church enumerates not only corporal works of mercy but spiritual works of mercy as well, and that the latter actually have a certain preeminence. Perhaps not everyone is ready to instruct the ignorant or admonish sinners. But at least one of the spiritual works of mercy is something that virtually all of us can do, regardless of our location or state of health: interceding for the living and the dead. Indeed, this is the work of mercy performed by the glorified saints in heaven.

3. Charity begins at home. That angel of mercy, Blessed Mother Teresa of Calcutta, was often approached by people who wanted to share in her apostolate to the poorest of the poor. Her advice to them was often to go home and love their own family members. If we open our eyes, there are people all around us who are lonely, sick, overworked, and troubled. They very much need our compassion and attention. This is where we must start. "If any one does not provide for his relatives, and especially for his own family, he has disowned the faith and is worse than an unbeliever" (1 Timothy 5:8).

4. Charity can't end at home. The story of the Good Samaritan is striking for a number of reasons, not the least of which is the fact that the hero of the story had no natural bond with the victim. Jews and Samaritans actually had great antipathy for each other. So we can't restrict our works of mercy to family, friends, and those who belong to our Church or political party. As Jesus tells us in the Sermon on the Mount, our works of mercy must extend even to our enemies.

5. Mercy is not always convenient. There are times that works of mercy can be planned and fit in an orderly way into our schedule. But suffering and crisis are often unpredictable. And responding to them can often be inconvenient. The Good Samaritan took a lot of time and went through no small expense to make sure the victim in the story was provided for. He was probably late for an appointment as a result.

6. Charity is not the same as social work. While people often refer to anything that benefits the disadvantaged as "charity," the word actually means divine, supernatural love. It is action that springs from the love of God that has been poured into our hearts by the Holy Spirit (see Romans 5:5) and must involve not just giving things but giving ourselves. We must see God's image and likeness in the person that benefits from our charity, and love that person for God's sake. There is nothing wrong with making a year-end charitable gift, but if this is to be a true work of mercy, the motivation must be deeper than the wish for a tax write-off. For St. Francis and Mother Teresa, serving the poorest of the poor was serving Jesus himself (see Matthew 25:34–46). A work of mercy can and should be a deeply spiritual encounter.

7. Mercy is never condescending. The goal of the ancient enemy of mankind is to use suffering to rob those made in God's image of their human dignity. Our goal in the work of mercy is always to restore that dignity and honor it. "Charity" that belittles the recipient is never true mercy. It may relieve some bodily suffering, but it only causes a deeper suffering of alienation and humiliation. The Divine Word emptied himself of glory and stood shoulder to shoulder with us. The one giving mercy cannot look down on the recipient of mercy. In fact, the merciful humbly understand that they always receive as much or more as they give when they work to alleviate the suffering of the needy.

St. John Paul wrote an encyclical on God the Father near the beginning of his pontificate. With all the possible descriptions and titles for God used in Scripture and Tradition, what was he to title such an encyclical? The answer for him was simple: "Rich in Mercy" (see Ephesians 2:4). God is preeminently the Father of mercies and the God of all consolation (see 2 Corinthians 1:3). The way we can be recognized as his authentic offspring is by living a lifestyle of mercy. It is interesting that in the Bible's only description of the last judgment, salvation or damnation hangs not on how much religious art people have in their houses or how many Masses they've attended, but how they've treated the least of Jesus's needy brothers and sisters (see Matthew 25:34–46).

SECOND SUNDAY OF LENT

The Transfiguration

Imagine: You are ten years past customary retirement age. It's time finally to kick back and relax. You live in a great city where everything is at your fingertips—shopping opportunities, cultural events, all your relatives and lifelong friends. Suddenly God appears and tells you to pack up, uproot your life, and march into an uncivilized wilderness.

This is what happens to Abram in Genesis 12. He lives in Mesopotamia, the cradle of civilization. He's seventy-five, and he's not getting any younger. He doesn't even know the name of the God who calls him.

Wouldn't you "discuss" this one a bit? Not Abram. Genesis reports no back-talk, no "yeah-buts." In a fit of understatement, Genesis simply says, "Abram went as the Lord directed him."

That's faith. Abram hears a command from a God he can't see, believes that this God must know what he is talking about, and begins a journey to he knows not where. Keep in mind that Paul says, "We walk by faith, not by sight" (2 Corinthians 5:7). That's why Abraham is the great model of faith in the Old Testament. Faith is not just about believing. It's about walking.

Obviously Abram's choice to walk involved great hardship. What was the motivation that drove him to do it? Simple. There was something that God promised him that he desperately wanted. He had a lot of things—a wife, property, servants, and all the creature comforts afforded by his civilization. Yet he lacked a son. And for a Semite like Abram who had no belief in any sort of afterlife, a son was the only ticket to immortality. A son would, presumably, go out and beget sons, thus keeping his father's name alive. God promised not only descendants but a progeny so numerous and so great that all the communities of the earth would find blessing in Abram's name.

Thus, it was desire for future glory that enabled Abram to put up with the hardships entailed in answering the call. This desire is called hope.

About nineteen hundred years later, St. Paul wrote these words to Timothy: "Bear your share of the hardship which the gospel entails" (2 Timothy 1:8). To be a Christian during the first three hundred years meant risking everything. If the Romans caught you, it could mean torture or death or—if you got off easy—the confiscation of all of your possessions. Why would people take this chance? For the same reason Abram embraced hardship: hope. They had been given a vision and a promise of eternal glory. They understood that no earthly good could compare with this everlasting joy and so were willing to suffer whatever loss necessary in order to secure it. In this, they followed their master, who "for the joy that was set before him endured the cross, despising the shame" (Hebrews 12:2).

Aware of the trauma the apostles would shortly suffer through the horror of his crucifixion, the Lord Jesus gave their leaders a vision of hope to sustain them. He went up on Mount Tabor and at last appeared as he really was (see Matthew 17:1–9). In anticipation of his risen glory, the Light of the World shone forth in the dazzling white of his divinity. The Law and the Prophets bore witness to him through Moses and Elijah. The Father's voice boomed the affirmation that this was indeed his beloved son. The Holy Spirit was manifested as the *shekinah*, the cloud of glory that had led the Israelites on their desert journey. This transfiguration is a scene that proclaims the whole Gospel, the Good News of a glorious life, won by the Savior, which would last forever.

But the experience itself did not last forever. It was not given to them so they could erect tents and stay there. There was still walking to do. The path called the Via Dolorosa lay before Jesus and before his followers as well. The experience called the Transfiguration was meant to show them that this way of the cross was not a road to death but through death to a life that makes even death seem but a trifle.

DAY 11

Watch Mel Gibson's movie The Passion of the Christ *during Lent or Holy Week and invite someone to watch it with you. Use* The Guide to the Passion: 100 Questions about the Passion of the Christ, *to facilitate discussion afterward.*

Appearances can be deceiving. After all, Jesus was just another Galilean. His hands were the rough hands of a workman. People in Nazareth knew his mother. Some even remembered the man they thought was his dad.

Yet when Jesus went up on Mt. Tabor with his three closest disciples, his appearance changed. The glory of his divinity suddenly became visible, shining through his humanity, dazzling his overwhelmed disciples (Luke 9:28–36).

But then two others showed up—Moses and Elijah. Of all the great figures of the Old Testament, why them? One reason is that the Jews were not abstract but rather very concrete thinkers. When they thought about the first five books of the Bible, "the Law" or "Torah," they thought of a person— Moses. When they considered the Bible's prophetic writings, the greatest prophet came to mind—Elijah. "The Law and the Prophets." That was the Jewish way of saying "the Bible." Moses and Elijah witness to Jesus because all of Scripture witnesses to him.

But what did the three of them talk about? His miracles? His teaching? Neither. They spoke about his "departure" soon to be accomplished in Jerusalem. This is what is predicted and described in a mysterious way all throughout the Law, the Prophets, and the Psalms—namely his march straight through indescribable suffering and death on his way to resurrected glory.

Troubling to many people when they think about Christ's passion are his words from the cross: "My God, my God, why have you forsaken me?" (Matthew 27:46). Some have even read into this a mistaken theology that Jesus, taking our place, experienced the most terrible consequence of our sin, namely being cut off from communion from the Father, separated from God and his grace. Not a chance. The fact that Jesus bore our sin cannot mean this.

He is not a sinner. His communion with the Father and the Spirit can never be interrupted. The cloud overshadowing the disciples at the Transfiguration was the same cloud of the Spirit that overshadowed Mary at the annunciation. The voice of the Father resounded forth from it. The Father and the Spirit were with him on Mt. Tabor. The Father and the Spirit were with him on Golgotha.

So how do we take Jesus's words? They are a quote from Psalm 22. In fact, the ancient Jewish practice was to designate a particular psalm not by a number but by its first few words (we still do this with conciliar documents such as *Lumen Gentium*). Make this psalm part of your meditation on the passion this Lent. In a remarkable way it predicts the mockery that is hurled upon Christ that fateful day, the piercing of his hands and feet by a pack of "dogs" (an uncomplimentary term used in those days to refer to Gentiles), the gambling for his clothing, even his eventual deliverance by the God who hears his cry. So Jesus, from the cross, is proclaiming what is manifest in the transfiguration: "All the law and the prophets bear witness to me and to what is happening right now."

This is why Jesus came. This is why for ten chapters in Luke's Gospel, Jesus is resolutely making his way towards Jerusalem (see Luke 9—19). His teaching and his miracles are remarkable. But if he had not laid down his life for us, if he had not been raised from the dead, we'd still be in our sins. The entire drama of human history finds its center and its meaning in these few tumultuous days.

Some have asked why Mel Gibson's movie was only about Jesus's passion, and not the entire life of Christ. This is the reason. Theologically, the page dividing the New and Old Testaments is not the golden-edged one between Malachi and Matthew, but rather the crimson-tinged page of the passion.

And if you've seen this movie, you understand why Peter, James, and John needed the glory of Tabor before enduring the horror of Golgotha.

DAY 12

Make a decision to read a portion of Scripture every day. Consider getting involved in a parish, online, or CD/DVD Bible study so as to learn more about God's Word. During special seasons such as Lent, the Mass readings are thematically coordinated and make for a fantastic Bible study! So get a Daily Missal, go online, or get a smartphone app such as Laudate or iMissal to follow the daily readings from Mass.

There is a myth that we must lay to rest, once and for all: Protestants are all about the Bible, while Catholics are all about the sacraments. While I can't speak for my Protestant brethren, I can say this with certainty: The Catholic Church has never tolerated any such "either/or." Both Scripture and the sacraments are precious gifts from the Lord, gifts we desperately need.

"Ignorance of Scripture is ignorance of Christ!"* insisted St. Jerome, a father and doctor of the Catholic Church from the fifth century A.D. Because of this, every liturgical service of the Catholic Church is full of Scripture. Take Sunday Mass, for instance. First there are significant chunks of Scripture read aloud, just as we see in Nehemiah 8 when the Torah was read to the people or in Luke 4:16–21 when Jesus serves as lector at the synagogue of Capernaum. But don't forget the prayers and acclamations that are full of Scripture like the Sanctus (a combination of Isaiah 6 and Psalm 118:26), the Our Father (see Matthew 6:9), and the Gloria (Luke 2:14).

So is hearing Scripture on Sunday enough? Not by a long shot. Scripture, says the Second Vatican Council (*Dei Verbum*, 21), is "food for the soul." Who eats just once a week? To survive and thrive, you need daily nourishment. You can have a steady diet of Scripture by attending Mass daily, participating in the Liturgy of the Hours, or reading Scripture in daily prayer. Actually, all three make an unbeatable combination.

Frequently, though, when Catholics start reading the Bible, they quickly run into trouble. Yes, sometimes it is hard to know where to begin, how to fit

* Letter from St. Jerome to Eustochium, http://epistolae.ccnmtl.columbia.edu/letter/273.html.

it all together, and how to interpret correctly some rather obscure passages, words, and names. My father, who first picked up the Bible at age sixty-three, discovered the book of Malachi. Thinking the name was pronounced "ma-LA-chee," he rejoiced that there was an Italian among the prophets.

There are great Catholic Bible studies found in books, on audios and videos, and on the Internet (see my website, dritaly.com, for suggestions and links). Some are book-by-book commentaries. Others are big-picture over-views of salvation history that help you fit each book, character, and theme into the overall story of God's dealings with his people. Most are conveniently designed so busy people with no background in the Bible can learn a lot without a huge time commitment.

Many of us spend sixteen or more years of our life preparing for our secular career, then take continuing education courses on nights or weekends. In contrast, how much have we invested in our education in the Word of God, essential for our heavenly career?

The study of the Bible is for one purpose, however: so that, praying with Scripture, we may be better able to understand what God is saying to us here and now. The writers of Sacred Scripture were inspired by the Holy Spirit. But it is equally true that the Scriptures themselves are inspired. The Holy Spirit has been "breathed into them" and resides within their words. When we approach the Scriptures prayerfully, aided by the same Spirit who dwells in them, reading Scripture becomes an experience of being filled and empow-ered by God's Spirit, and we are changed.

Sometimes the words of Scripture are encouraging. For instance, St. Paul in 1 Corinthians 12 tells us that no matter how insignificant we may feel, we each have an essential role to play as members of the body of Christ. But other times Scripture holds a mirror up to our face and we don't like what we see. In Nehemiah 8, the people wept at the reading of the Word, because it made them realize their sin. The Word is truth, and sometimes the truth is painful. But so is antiseptic on a wound. Scripture challenges us only to heal us and call us to growth. No pain, no gain.

DAY 13

Do you know anyone preparing for baptism or confirmation at the Easter Vigil? If not, find out who is going through RCIA in your parish and spiritually "adopt" at least one person, offering your Lenten penance in intercession for that person and all those preparing to enter into full communion with the Church at Easter.

Lent is a time of introspection. In Exodus, we watch the Israelites grumbling, even after the amazing things God had done for them (Exodus 17:3–7). In them, we recognize ourselves. For many of us, then, Lent is time for the spiritual equivalent of New Year's resolutions. We work on ourselves for forty days so we don't end up wandering around in the wilderness for forty years. We do things to burn off the fat that has been weighing us down; we try to improve our spiritual diet, and we do some spiritual exercises to strengthen the muscles we call "virtues."

But in the early days of the Church, Lent was not so much a time to focus inward. It was a time for Christians to focus outward. It was a time not just for personal growth, but for growth of the Church.

In the days of the Church fathers, did the whole Church fast, pray, and give alms for the forty days preceding Easter? Absolutely. But Christians did this primarily for the sake of others. There were two groups of people that were the main beneficiaries of this prayer and penance: new Christians to be baptized at Easter and lapsed Catholics to be readmitted to communion. These folks were praying and fasting during Lent to break the power of darkness and prepare themselves to cross the Jordan into the Promised Land.

We ought to recover this ancient tradition and do penance for and with those who will enter or return to the Church at Easter. But there is something else that we should do. There are millions more who should be returning or entering. We need to tell them about Jesus.

"Evangelize? That's not my charism, not my personality." "I need more education first." "I evangelize by example." But the second Vatican Council and all the popes since teach that all are called to evangelize in both deed and word.

True, not everyone is a Fulton Sheen or a Billy Graham, and not everyone can manage to get a degree in theology. But the story of the Samaritan woman (see John 4) teaches the kind of evangelism that all of us can manage.

First, Jesus modeled it for us. He came to a town where everyone was a member of a heretical sect, and he sat down by a well. A woman came to draw water. Israelites usually didn't talk to Samaritans, much less drink out of their vessels (which were considered ritually impure). To boot, men usually didn't make conversation with women. But Jesus recognized this woman's existence and affirmed her by being willing to accept a drink from her. Once she got over her shock, a dialogue ensued. It started out with them talking about water, wells, Jews, and Samaritans, but then Jesus asked her questions that threw her off a bit and make her think. He finally asked a question that led her to "fess up" and admit her need. She's hungry for love, and had run through quite a few partners looking for the real thing. Jesus's soul-piercing glance tells her that his is the love she's been looking for. She abandoned her water jar and returned to the city to tell everyone about Jesus.

Did she wait until she had a master's degree in theology? Did she sit down with people and demonstrate from Scripture why he was the Messiah? No. She simply told people, with joy, confidence, and conviction, what Jesus had done for her. And she invited people to come and experience him for themselves.

And that's how a large portion of that heretical town came to believe. That's how a large portion of the Roman Empire came to believe. There were no stadium crusades, no TV preachers. Christians simply listened to their neighbors and coworkers with respect and love, asked questions to find out their needs, and told them how Jesus had met similar needs in their lives. And then an invitation was issued to come check it out.

One of our Lenten resolutions this year ought to be to get over our fear of sharing the Good News, to be aware of the spiritual needs of those around us, and to share God's love. More people are looking than you think. "The fields are already white for harvest" (John 4:35).

DAY 14

Sometime during the week, visit a local church and spend some time in Eucharistic Adoration. It doesn't matter if the Eucharist is exposed in the monstrance or hidden in the tabernacle; prayer in the presence of the Blessed Sacrament is powerful. Stay for at least thirty minutes if you can.

If you haven't noticed, the traditional practice of Eucharistic Adoration is making a comeback. Many were given the impression in the 1970s that Adoration was passé, a relic of pre-Vatican II spirituality. But all the popes since the Council have emphasized its importance, and we see more and more parishes organizing regular, even perpetual, exposition and Adoration.

But what do you do when praying before the Blessed Sacrament? First, let me point out what *not* to do. There are two extremes to avoid. At one end of the spectrum is hyper-busyness. This happens when a person feels so uncomfortable with quiet that he or she fills up every minute of adoration with nonstop reading or talking to God; this leaves no room for silent attentiveness to God's voice. The other extreme I've encountered is the idea that it's inappropriate to do anything except gaze on the Eucharist and be still. The problem here is that most of us aren't equipped to walk in from our busy life, sit still, and be focused. Our minds are everywhere but on the presence of the Lord.

So how does one pray before the Blessed Sacrament? Since Eucharistic Adoration is essentially a matter of lingering over the mystery of the Mass in a prolonged moment of contemplation, everything that happens at Mass is appropriate to do during Adoration. In fact, Church documents on the subject teach that we should take the Mass as our guide.

Notice that at Mass, we don't jump into Communion right away. We prepare ourselves with repentance, with listening to God's Word in Scripture, with offering praise and thanks in prayers like the Gloria and the Eucharistic Prayer. We intercede for the needs of all. Finally, we receive the Lord and rest in his presence, giving ourselves to him and enjoying a deep union with him.

Each of these types of prayer is suitable for our times before the Blessed Sacrament. Certainly, there's no obligation to use them all or follow the exact sequence in which they appear in the Mass. At the same time, our Adoration should culminate as the Mass does, with simple resting in the arms of the Lord.

Silently repeating a word or short phrase can be a great aid in keeping us focused as we gaze on the Lord. One great tradition in the Church is to repeat the name of Jesus or the well-known Jesus Prayer: "Jesus Christ, Son of God, have mercy on me." Also, certain Scriptures are especially effective in helping us recall that we're in the Lord's magnificent presence. One of my favorites is Psalm 46:10: "Be still, and know that I am God." Another is Psalm 63, which speaks of thirsting and pining for God as in "a dry and weary land" and goes on to evokes the joy of gazing on God "in the sanctuary" and being filled, as with a banquet (Psalm 63:1–8). This, of course, is truly what happens in Adoration: It's a spiritual communion that fills our soul, as with a banquet.

For me, Adoration is like spiritual sunbathing: I put myself in the presence of the Lord and allow myself to bask in the healthful rays of the Sun of Righteousness. I've spent many moments in Adoration over the years and have received tremendous grace and healing of some significant wounds. The Lord has also used these times to guide me in some remarkable ways. It was in front of the Blessed Sacrament that I discovered my vocation to become a theologian.

I must also confess that there have been many times when my adoration has wandered off into daydreams, distractions, and even sleep! Not every moment before the Blessed Sacrament is glorious, I've discovered, but if you persevere, you will have moments when the Lord touches you profoundly. Those times make all the struggles worthwhile.

DAY 15

Make the Confiteor a daily prayer during Lent, and recite it in the morning or before bed.

> *I confess to almighty God and to you, my brothers and sisters,*
> *that I have greatly sinned in my thoughts and in my words,*
> *in what I have done and in what I have failed to do,*
> *through my fault, through my fault, through my most grievous*
>   *fault;*
> *therefore I ask blessed Mary ever-Virgin, all the Angels and Saints,*
> *and you, my brothers and sisters, to pray for me to the Lord our*
>   *God.*

Finally, I was old enough to be an altar boy. The liturgy was still in Latin, and I worked hard to memorize those Latin prayers. I have to admit, we altar boys would compete with each other to see who could rattle off the prayers faster. But one prayer forced us to put the brakes on for at least a minute. Near the beginning of the Mass, we would slow down and dramatically say, "*Mea culpa, mea culpa, mea maxima culpa,*" beating our breast with our fist at each repetition of the phrase. "Through my fault, through my fault, through my most grievous fault."

No sooner had my serving career begun than the rules changed. Due to something the priest called "Vatican II," we began saying the *Confiteor* in English and were disappointed that the threefold "mea culpa" had disappeared.

In the revised 2011 English translation of the Mass, the threefold refrain reappeared, and we are once again encouraged to symbolically strike our breasts each time we acknowledge our fault.

Why was this restored? And why do we, at the beginning of the prayer, not only admit that we have sinned, but that we have *greatly* sinned?

The first reason is that the Catholic Mass is thoroughly biblical. So let's start by noting what a threefold repetition means in the Jewish mentality. In

Hebrew, you can't add endings to words to express superlatives or emphasis. There is no "big, bigger, biggest" in the language of the Old Testament. So how do you get the idea across that something is the best, worst, or extremely important? By repeating it three times. When Isaiah had a vision of the Lord attended by angels, they cried out, "Holy, Holy, Holy!" which we repeat at every Mass. Peter's denied Jesus three times. The Lord later asked Peter, "Do you love me?" (John 21:15–17) not once, but three times.

Therefore, a threefold admission of our fault is a biblical way to emphasize what is said at the start of the prayer—that we have "greatly" sinned. Sin is not just a casual affair, an inconsequential blunder like failing to dot an *i* or cross a *t*. Sin is a most serious matter. God has given us everything, even sacrificing his only Son for us. He deserves all our love, as we say in the act of contrition. We are commanded to love him with all of our heart, soul, mind, and strength. When we fail to do so by neglecting our duty or by doing something that hurts others, ourselves, and God's honor, it is grievous. As we become aware of what we've done or failed to do, the proper response is contrition, the kind of sorrow that leads not to despair but to change.

But why the striking of our breasts as we recall our fault? Is being Catholic all about beating ourselves up? For the answer, we again need to turn to the Scriptures. In Luke 18:9-14, we meet a very pious Pharisee who congratulates God on being so fortunate as to have such a worthy servant as himself. There is also a publican, a tax collector, who strikes his breast as he comes before the Lord saying, "Lord, be merciful to me, a sinner."

By striking our breast, we distance ourselves from the Pharisee and stand, or rather bow, with the publican, acknowledging our unworthiness before the awesome majesty and perfect holiness of the living God. It is not about self-hatred but about humility. And humility means getting in touch with reality. As we begin the liturgy, we pause to recall that we don't deserve to be there. We are all publicans and prodigals whom a loving Father embraces and welcomes not because of our virtues but in spite of our sins.

DAY 16

Instead of secular films for weekend entertainment, try some movies that will enrich your spiritual life—such as A Man for All Seasons *(about St. Thomas More), or* Jesus of Nazareth *by Franco Zeffirelli.*

Some think Lent is a time for fasting. I see it as a time of feasting.

I come to this conclusion based on the story of the fig tree in Luke 13. Three years without bearing fruit.... What could be the problem? The owner figures that it is simply a dud and wants to cut it down. The vinedresser, a little more in touch with nature, comes to a different conclusion. Maybe all that is needed to turn things around is a bit of fertilizer.

As we look at Christians in America, we have to be honest. Over three-quarters of us say we are Christians. So where's the fruit? We're certainly feeding ourselves often enough, seeing that 70 percent of Americans are over-weight. Obviously what we're consuming is not quite the right nourishment to produce the desired results.

So Lent is a time to examine our diet and make some changes. First, let's cut out the junk food that bloats us. It could be the chips, fries, burgers, and sodas that drain our pocketbooks and make us lethargic. Or it could be too many hours of radio, TV, and social media—which fill our heads with so much noise that we can't sit still, quiet down, and listen to God. Let's turn it all off for a while.

Yes, this is fasting. But the goal is to save our appetite so that we can feast on other things such as the Word of God. When is the last time you sat down and read an entire book of the Bible from start to finish (if not all in one sitting, over the course of a few days)? Exodus makes for a good Lenten read, since 1 Corinthians 10 tells us that Israel's odyssey was for our sake, to provide an example. When was the last time you identified a short, poignant Bible text and memorized it, repeating it daily, or even several times a day, meditating on it and applying it to various aspects of your life?

How about the Eucharist, the greatest nourishment of all? Lent is a great time to go more often, even daily. Adoration of the Blessed Sacrament outside of Mass is like stimulating the appetite before the meal (*aperitif*) or taking time to digest it afterward (*digestif*). Either way, Adoration helps us derive more benefit from our Eucharistic feast.

Then there is the time we devote to entertainment. Could we not redirect some of those hours to entertainment that nourishes our spiritual life? Mel Gibson's film on the Lord's passion was released on Ash Wednesday for a reason. It was offered as a Lenten meditation to help us understand the shocking consequences of sin and the astounding Love that lays down his life for his friends. If you fear that the violence of *The Passion of The Christ* would be too much for you, get Franco Zeffirelli's *Jesus of Nazareth,* and watch it with family and friends. If you prefer books, read the life of a saint or the powerful religious fiction of an author such as C.S. Lewis.

Finally, one of the most spiritually nourishing and energizing experiences of all is giving of ourselves. We call this almsgiving. It is in giving that we receive, says the Prayer of St. Francis. If we save money from fasting, let's give it away. There are the corporal works of mercy such as feeding the hungry. Then there are the spiritual works of mercy, such as feeding the spiritually hungry, the millions of nominal Christians and unchurched people that starve to death for lack of the Word of God. Soup kitchens and evangelization ministries both need our support.

Prayer. Fasting. Almsgiving. Three interrelated fertilizers to help the barren fig tree bear fruit. But keep in mind the owner's directive: Fertilize it for a year, and if there are no results, fetch the axe. So, no more excuses. No more procrastinating. Let's vow to make this Lent count. There may not be another.

The Cleansing of the Temple and the Ten Commandments

When it started, all was fresh and new. An unnamed but mighty God freed a motley crew of slaves and offered them a new way of life in a new land. Most importantly, he offered them a privileged and exclusive relationship with himself.

In the ancient world, most nations worshipped their own god and believed themselves to have a special claim on his favor. The Greeks had Zeus and the Canaanites, Ba'al, for instance. But this was different. This mysterious God called himself "I AM WHO AM" and apparently tolerated no rivals. He had beaten the Egyptian gods on their own turf and appeared ready to take his new people into Ba'al's territory. None of the other gods required any special behavior, just sacrificial worship. This new one required fidelity to a code of conduct that reached into every department of life, not just the religious. No area was off limits to the claims of this God—economics, family life, even sexuality. If Israel wanted this special relationship, they had to accept the stamp of his ownership on every aspect of their existence. That was the real meaning of the Ten Commandments.

But what began with heartfelt zeal ultimately became ritual routine. The code of the covenant had called for animal sacrifices and a special place to carry them out. The devotion of David demanded a fitting place for God's house. The resourcefulness of his shrewd son Solomon made the dream a reality. After the Babylonians destroyed the Temple, it was rebuilt in tears, a shadow of its former self. Then a powerful king came along who saw an opportunity to make the temple once again the pride of God's people. He rebuilt it in even greater glory. But it was more a monument to himself than to God. After all, he cared little for God and was not even himself a full-blooded Jew. He was, rather, a cold-blooded murderer whose name will forever live in infamy: Herod the Great.

How about the religious leaders of Herod's day? For them, religion had become a business. Animals were needed for sacrifice, so they were sold in the Temple precincts. Special currency was needed for the payment of the Temple tax, so moneychangers were conveniently available for people to exchange their Roman money for the appropriate coinage.

The prophet Malachi (see 3:1–5) predicted that the Lord would suddenly come to his Temple to deal with such things. And Zechariah 14:21 foretold that on the day of the Lord, there would no longer be any merchant in the Temple precincts.

So when Jesus overturned the moneychangers' tables (John 2:13–25), he was fulfilling Scripture and making clear that the messianic time was at hand. No more business as usual. No more ho-hum approach to religion. It was now time for living faith, not just religious belief. Zeal for God's house consumed him, and he was determined to light the fire of zeal in us as well.

Lent provides us with an opportunity for a gut check. Has our religion become a cold routine, a mere collection of intellectual convictions and external rituals, as with the scribes and Pharisees? Is our piety more a monument to ourselves than to God, as in the case of Herod? Is Christ crucified the power and the wisdom of God, or just a plaster figure hanging on the wall?

The story of Jesus and the moneychangers comes at the beginning of the Gospel of John. From the very outset of his public ministry, Jesus predicted his death and resurrection to his uncomprehending audience. It would be his self-sacrifice that would ultimately lead to a new beginning. And to prepare for that event, he cleaned house.

As we prepare for the celebration of the mystery of redemption, it is time for us, too, to clean house and honor Christ's self-sacrifice with authentic sacrifices of our own.

DAY 17

Pledge to recite the Our Father every day, slowly and thoughtfully. Try to do it three times per day—morning, midday, and evening.

The major world religions have been around for a long time. Most believe in one God. All teach the gist of the Ten Commandments.

But in a few respects, Christianity is absolutely unique. That the supreme Being is not just "King of the Universe" or "Master" but "Father." That he desires a close, familiar relationship with us—this you don't find anywhere outside the teaching of Jesus.

This shocking intimacy with the Galaxy Maker is made possible only by Christ's death and resurrection. Through faith and baptism, our old self, cut off from God, dies with Christ on the cross. We begin a new life in Christ. "It is no longer I who live, but it is Christ who lives in me" (Galatians 2:20). Jesus shares everything with us, since we are now members of his body. He shares his own righteousness with us, so we are forgiven for every one of our sins (see Colossians 2:13–14). He even shares his Father with us. Thus, when he teaches us to pray (see Luke 11:1–4; Matthew 6:9–13), we're told to address God as he does, as "Abba."

To call God "Father" does not mean to say, of course, that he is an old man with a white beard. Only the second person of the Blessed Trinity wedded himself to a male human nature in the womb of Mary. The Father and the Holy Spirit are pure spirit and transcend male and female, masculine and feminine (see *CCC* 239). This is no new insight brought to Christianity by the feminist movement. It has always been taught that the word *Father* applied to God is used by way of analogy. Analogies tell us something very true despite being imperfect. Until recently, the father was recognized by Western society as the origin, head, and provider of the family. To call the first person of the Trinity "Father" means that he is the origin and transcendent authority of all and cares for the needs of all.

But we all instinctively know that a father who pays the bills and barks orders is not enough. We expect a dad to have an intimate, affectionate relationship with his children, to spend "quality time" with them. To call God "Father" means, then, that he is near to us, intimately concerned with us, fond of us, even crazy about us. He is not the distant clockmaker God of Thomas Jefferson and the Deists. This aloof God of the philosophers created the world to run on its own so that he could withdraw and occupy himself with more interesting pursuits.

No, the God whom Jesus calls Father cares about us and knows us intimately. "Every hair on your head is numbered" (Matthew 10:30). He tells us to ask him for "our daily bread," which stands for all that we need to grow physically and spiritually. Luke's version of the Lord's Prayer in Luke 11:2–4 leaves out "Thy will be done," but it is implied in "Thy kingdom come." God's kingdom means God having his way, not necessarily us getting our way. Sometimes God gives us exactly what we ask for because this corresponds with what is best for us and everybody else (his will always involves this). But we know that sometimes our kids ask for things that may be appealing at first glance but really are ultimately not in their best interest. Abraham asked that Sodom be spared for the sake of the innocent. But God saw that it would be best to get Abraham's righteous cousins out of Sodom and destroy the city to protect humanity from its predatory violence. Abraham got what he really wanted, but not the way he wanted it (Genesis 18:20ff).

God wants us to pray relentlessly for our needs and the needs of others. He is always listening. But he listens beyond our words to hear the true desire of our hearts. And that is what he gives us. It may come wrapped in some unexpected packaging. And it may take some time. But it comes. After all, he is our Father.

DAY 18

Forgive those who have offended you or your loved ones. In fact, think of the person who has most hurt you or most annoys you. Spend several minutes each day thanking God for that person and asking God to bless him or her.

Just about everyone can recite the Lord's Prayer from memory. That's precisely the problem, though. We often rattle it off without really thinking about what we are saying.

"Forgive us our trespasses as we forgive those who trespass against us." Whenever we pray this line, we are asking God to forgive us in exactly the same way as we forgive those who hurt us. In other words, if we are harboring unforgiveness in our hearts as we say this prayer, we are calling a curse down upon ourselves.

Let's face it, we are all in desperate need of the mercy of God. But time and time again, the Word of God makes clear that the greatest block to his mercy is resentment. In the Old Testament, Sirach 27:30—28:7 tells us how wrath and anger, cherished and held tight, are poisons that lead to spiritual death. Jesus thinks this is so important that he includes a reminder of this lesson in the central prayer that he teaches to his disciples. And to drive the point home, he tells us the parable of the merciless servant, recorded in the Gospel of Matthew (see 18:21–35). As we listen to the story, we are incensed at the arrogance and hard-heartedness of someone who is forgiven a huge debt yet immediately throttles the neighbor who owes him a fraction of the amount he himself once owed. Incensed, that is, until we realize the story is about us. For all of us who have ever nurtured a grudge are guilty of exactly the same thing.

Bringing up this issue is rather uncomfortable, because we all have been hurt by others. Many have been hurt deeply. Think, for example, of the widows and orphans of September 11. Is it wrong to have feelings of outrage over such crimes? Does forgiveness mean that we excuse the culprits and leave ourselves wide open to further abuse?

Not at all. First of all, forgiveness is a decision, not a feeling. I think it rather unlikely that the Lord Jesus, in his sacred yet still human heart, had tender feelings of affection for those mocking him as his blood was being drained out on the cross. But he made a decision, expressed in a prayer: "Father, forgive them, for they know not what they do" (Luke 23:34). In other words, there was no vindictiveness, no desire to retaliate and cause pain, suffering, and destruction to those who delighted in causing him pain. Such desire for destructive vengeance is the kind of anger mentioned as one of the seven deadly sins. Instead, Jesus prayed to the Father for their good even as they caused him harm.

Did Jesus ever experience anger against those who sought his life? Absolutely. Righteous anger is the appropriate response to injustice. It is intended to give us the emotional energy to confront that injustice and overcome it. Recall how livid Jesus was in the face of the Pharisees' hypocrisy, because it was blocking access to his life-giving truth. But notice as well that he overturned the moneychangers' tables, not their lives.

Forgiveness does not mean being a doormat. It does not mean sitting passively by while an alcoholic or abusive family member destroys not only your life but the lives of others. But taking severe, even legal action does not require resentment and vindictiveness. St. John Paul II did not request the release of the man who shot him. But he visited him in prison to offer him forgiveness and friendship. In so doing, he stunned not only his assailant but the whole world.

Develop your relationship with St. Joseph, the often forgotten foster father of Jesus. Ask him daily to join with you in praying for all the important fathers in your life, including the Holy Father, your bishops and all bishops, the priests and deacons of your parish, and all priests and deacons.

In the drama of the incarnation, Jesus is, of course, the star. That's the way it is at every birth. All eyes are on the baby. The costar, though, is definitely Mom. Without her love and labor, the event could not have happened. In this case, without Mom's faith, it couldn't have happened either. According to Luke's Gospel, an angel brought Mary stunning news. She believed the unbelievable and said, "Let it be."

But there is a best supporting actor in the drama as well. True, Joseph was not the biological father, but the messiah had to be of David's royal line. In ancient Israel, a child's clan was determined by that of his father. So it was Joseph who legally bound Jesus to the house of David. It was because of Joseph that the family had to go to Bethlehem for the census, so that the prophecy might be fulfilled.

God carefully selected the woman who would be the mother of his Son. But he must have been equally careful in his selection of the foster father. Genes are not the only thing parents impart to their children. Jesus, in his humanity, had to grow in wisdom, age, and grace (see Luke 2:52). Joseph must have been responsible for a good deal of this growth. It was Joseph who was Jesus's male role model. From Joseph, Jesus learned many things, including the carpentry trade that he would practice for some twenty years.

But there are even more important things that Jesus learned from Joseph. Joseph was a just man, an honest man, a courageous man, a man of integrity. His betrothed was pregnant but not by him. Imagine the shame, the hurt, and the anger he must have experienced, assuming what anyone would assume in such a situation. His integrity would not allow him to marry an adulteress and pretend that the child was his. Neither would he expose the woman he loved to shame and punishment. He did not procrastinate or waffle. He made the difficult decision to divorce Mary quietly.

But then came the messenger. In Luke's Gospel, there was an angelic annunciation to Mary. In the first chapter of Matthew, we learn that Joseph gets one, too. He was named after the greatest dreamer of the Old Testament. Maybe that's why his annunciation came in a dream.

Mary's great claim to fame is her faith. When told the unbelievable, she believed.

Joseph's claim to fame is also his faith. He, too, was told the unbelievable and dared to believe. His response of faith entailed taking action—he changed his plans, received Mary into his home, and accepted responsibility for this special child. Keep this in mind, though: Mary needed no revelation to be sure this was a virginal conception. All Joseph had to go by was what he received from an angel, in a dream.

Do you think he may have been tempted at some point to second-guess this experience? Especially when things did not go smoothly—after all, when a plan is from God, are not doors supposed to open? Yet when Mary and Joseph arrived in Bethlehem, the door of the inn was slammed in their face. If this were God's child, wouldn't God provide a room? And if this were really God's son, wouldn't God have turned back Herod's hit men?

Then the angel shows up again in another dream: "Flee to Egypt with Mary and the baby."

Wasn't the seventy-mile walk to Bethlehem with a pregnant woman enough? If this was God's doing, shouldn't there be an easier way?

Joseph may or may not have thought these things. I would have. The point is, Joseph believed and acted. And when the angel came a third time and told him to make the long trek back to Nazareth, he acted again.

Joseph certainly did a lot of walking. From Nazareth to Bethlehem to Egypt and back again. Paul said we walk by faith, not by sight. Joseph is a model of faith because he keeps walking, even in the dark.

DAY 20

Plan a contemplative retreat this Lent. It could be simply half a day, out in nature or in a Church. Or it could be a full day. Or an overnight or two. You can certainly read lots of things during your retreat or listen to lots of talks. But try sticking mostly to Scripture, the liturgy, nature, and quiet as much as possible. During or at the end of the retreat, write down what the Holy Spirit seems to be saying to you—Scriptures that he brought to your attention, decisions or resolutions you made, and so on. Check out the retreat format in the Appendix; it was designed for Holy Week but would be appropriate all throughout Lent.

For many, the words "contemplative life" conjure up images of robed monks in choir stalls or veiled nuns behind metal grates. A chosen few of these sequestered people appear to be favored with revelations from on high. These we call mystics.

Since most of us are called to an active life, we assume that we are disqualified from contemplation. And to think we could be mystics would be simply an act of pride—or worse, an indication that we might need psychiatric help.

But if we look a bit deeper into the Catholic tradition, we see that contemplative, mystical prayer is actually a normal part of the Christian life meant to be experienced by everyone. Certainly there are religious orders especially dedicated to contemplation. But there are also orders, like the Missionaries of Charity, especially dedicated to works of mercy. Does that mean that the rest of us can forget about mercy? Special vocations like these exist to be a perpetual reminder to all of us of something we, too, are called to be and do.

If we look into both the Old and New Testaments, we see very active people called by God to special moments of contemplative prayer. Moses spent forty days and nights with God on Mt. Sinai. Elijah encountered God in a still, small voice and found restoration and renewed vision. The Lord Jesus himself often withdrew to spend hours in prayer.

But the best example of contemplation in the midst of action is the story of Martha and Mary (see Luke 10:38–42). Jesus comes to visit. Martha fusses. Mary stops, sits at his feet, and listens. She gives him her undivided attention.

This is our part in making contemplative prayer happen. We simply make ourselves available to God and focus on his presence. And his presence is most intensely experienced in two ways: through his inspired Word, and in the sacrament of his Body and Blood. Contemplative life is suspended between two poles, the Bible and the Eucharist.

To focus on God's presence is easier said than done. In every age, the necessary chores of everyday life—earning a living, homemaking, parenting, relationships—have a tendency to completely absorb us if we let them. This was Martha's problem.

Yet we have an additional obstacle that Martha did not have: modern media, which invades every nook and cranny of our lives. In various schools and seminars around the world, future advertising execs, graphic artists, and filmmakers are taught how to get our attention, keep our attention, and put tunes and images in our minds that just won't go away. They get to us through radio in the car, TV at home, even wireless Internet access all hours of the day and night wherever we are. We can shop either in stores or online 24/7— no break for Sundays and holidays. Organized activities abound for all ages. When I was a child aged nine to twelve, I walked to a field to play Little League baseball each spring. Now kids start sports before they can read and play two to three sports year round with summer tournaments that require parents to drive all over creation. Modern life has magnified the distraction factor. The potential for a frenetic, scattered lifestyle has never been greater.

Of course this kind of constant overstimulation takes its toll on the body as well as the soul. We need moments of contemplation to survive and thrive amidst this craziness. In an interesting study, praying the rosary was shown to lower blood pressure. It's just common sense.

So how to live a contemplative life in a society that never rests? We simply look at some activities and "just say no." That's what Mary did, much to Martha's chagrin. We may irk a family member, a friend, or a coworker. They'll cope! Limit TV viewing. Limit the number of activities you or your family engage in. When you get a few quiet moments, break the habit of turning on the radio or picking up a sales catalogue. Make some space for God.

OK, but now what do you do with the room you've created? Here are some practical ideas on how busy people can grow in the contemplative life:

1. Daily Quiet Time: We should offer up quick prayers to God throughout the day. But contemplative life demands a daily discipline of giving God undivided attention. If you are not currently doing this, try starting with fifteen minutes and gradually expand it to twenty to thirty minutes. An entire "holy hour" would be fabulous, though perhaps not possible for everyone. But it's the regularity more than the exact duration that's important. Find the best time for you. For me, it's early in the morning, before the rest of the household is up and the phones start ringing.

2. Adoration: Adoration is, according to an important Vatican document, "holding the Mass in a moment of contemplation."* It is unpacking and savoring the meaning of the entire Eucharistic liturgy. We are meant to have a few moments of silent contemplation after Communion at each Mass. But we can prolong this all throughout the week by spending time in quiet before the tabernacle. We can commit to a certain hour if our parish happens to have organized Adoration. Or we can simply go as we can and spend anywhere from a few minutes to an hour or more resting in the presence of the Lord. "Be still and know that I am God" (Psalm 46:10).

3. Rosary: "Mystical" prayer is pondering and uniting ourselves to the "mystery" of Christ's love expressed in his incarnation, ministry, death, and resurrection. The rosary, then, is by nature a mystical or contemplative prayer, if we pray it correctly. The vocal prayers are meant to help us "keep time" as we ponder the joyful, luminous, sorrowful, and glorious mysteries. Five decades of the rosary take about twenty minutes to pray. If you don't have that much time, say a decade or two at a time as your schedule allows.

4. *Lectio Divina*: This contemplative approach to Scripture was first developed by monks in the early days of the Church. They selected a small portion of Scripture, read it, and reread it slowly. They memorized it, pondered it, and chewed on it continuously as a cow chews the cud in order to extract all

---

* Marcellino D'Ambrosio, "Contemplation for Busy People," www.crossroadsinitiative.com.

the nourishment they could from it, assimilate it, and be transformed by it. Then they used it as a springboard to an intimate prayer of union with God, who inspired the text. Such a form of prayer with Scripture they called "divine reading" or "*lectio divina*." The Focolare movement of spiritual renewal has the practice of choosing one Scripture text and meditating on it continuously for a week in this way.

5. Liturgy of the Hours: The Church's Liturgy of the Hours may be sung by monks in choir stalls, but it is for everybody. Psalms and Scripture readings are organized in a four-week cycle for morning, midday, evening, and night prayer, with special readings and prayers for the various liturgical seasons and saints' days. You can get a one-volume abbreviated version (called *Christian Prayer*) or the full, four-volume version. Or you can get it online from various websites such as universalis.com or liturgyhours.org. You can even get it on your smartphone with applications such as Laudate or iBreviary.

6. Nature Walk: God's creation is a reflection of his glory. To unplug from the media and quietly walk amidst God's creation often helps to de-stress, dial-down, and dispose us for prayer. In fact, many of the psalms are great to read on a nature walk—try Psalm 19 on the occasion of a beautiful sky or Psalm 93 when the surf gets rough at the ocean.

7. Sunday: In his letter on restoring Sunday as the day of the Lord, St. John Paul II called Sunday a contemplative day. It is a time to avoid unnecessary work and chores, put away the to-do lists, and remember the salvation that Christ won for us through his crucifixion and resurrection. It's not just another day to catch up and get things done, but a day to pause and give thanks for what's already been accomplished for us and through us.

8. Retreats: Prayer is like breathing. We must do it continually. But sometimes you need to pause and take a really deep breath. That's what a retreat is for. It could be a weekend, an overnight, or even just a whole morning in front of the Blessed Sacrament. The important thing is that it is a good chunk of time dedicated to renewing and deepening our relationship with the Lord, away from the hustle and bustle of day-to-day life. There are many organized retreat programs that we can tap into through our parish, but it is also fine to go away alone with a Bible and a rosary and just be with God. If you have never done this, I challenge you to try it. You'll be surprised at how fast the time goes and how powerfully the Lord will speak to you.

DAY 21

Get to know the Fathers of the Church and read selections from them along with Scripture. (My book When the Church Was Young: The Voices of the Early Fathers *is a readable introduction.) Short selections from the Fathers' writings on Lenten themes, such as the one that follows, can be downloaded for free from the Lenten library at dritaly.com.*

This excellent reflection on one of the three pillars of Lenten penance, almsgiving or generosity, is an excerpt from a sermon on the love of poverty by St. Gregory Nazianzen.* Gregory was a wealthy member of the landed gentry before he became bishop. He practiced what he preached and gave his family fortune away to relieve the suffering of the poor.

> Recognize to whom you owe the fact that you exist, that you breathe, that you understand, that you are wise, and, above all, that you know God and hope for the kingdom of heaven and the vision of glory, now darkly as in a mirror but then with greater fullness and purity. You have been made a son of God, co-heir with Christ. Where did you get all this, and from whom?
>
> Let me turn to what is of less importance: the visible world around us. What benefactor has enabled you to look out upon the beauty of the sky, the sun in its course, the circle of the moon, the countless number of stars, with the harmony and order that are theirs, like the music of a harp? Who has blessed you with rain, with the art of husbandry, with different kinds of food, with the arts, with houses, with laws, with states, with a life of humanity and culture, with friendship and the easy familiarity of kinship?
>
> Who has given you dominion over animals, those that are tame and those that provide you with food? Who has made you lord and master of everything on earth? In short, who has endowed you with all that makes man superior to all other living creatures?

* Oratio 14, *De Pauperum amore*, 23-25: PG 35, 887–890.

Is it not God who asks you now in your turn to show yourself generous above all other creatures and for the sake of all other creatures? Because we have received from him so many wonderful gifts, will we not be ashamed to refuse him this one thing only, our generosity? Though he is God and Lord he is not afraid to be known as our Father. Shall we for our part repudiate those who are our kith and kin?

Brethren and friends, let us never allow ourselves to misuse what has been given us by God's gift. If we do, we shall hear St. Peter say: Be ashamed of yourselves for holding on to what belongs to someone else. Resolve to imitate God's justice, and no one will be poor. Let us not labor to heap up and hoard riches while others remain in need....

Let us put into practice the supreme and primary law of God. He sends down rain on just and sinful alike, and causes the sun to rise on all without distinction. To all earth's creatures he has given the broad earth, the springs, the rivers and the forests. He has given the air to the birds, and the waters to those who live in the water. He has given abundantly to all the basic needs of life, not as a private possession, not restricted by law, not divided by boundaries, but as common to all, amply and in rich measure. His gifts are not deficient in any way, because he wanted to give equality of blessing to equality of worth, and to show the abundance of his generosity.

Invite someone who doesn't regularly attend Mass to come to church with you sometime during Lent. It could be an inactive Catholic, a Christian from another church, someone from a non-Christian faith such as Islam, or an unchurched person with no religion.

This Lent, we are being asked not just to deepen our faith but to share it. It is finally time to take seriously the call to the New Evangelization and make it a part of our Lenten journey.

There are many churchgoing Catholics who experience the practice of their faith more as a chore than a joy. There are an increasing number of Catholics who have been away for a long time. And there are many from other religious traditions and of no religious background at all who don't know that they have a loving Father.

Evangelization is not about pushing our ideas on people. It's about letting them know the Good News that they are loved and forgiven, that their life has more meaning and promise than they ever suspected.

Several years ago, I called a cab to take me to the airport. I decided to make conversation with the driver who was obviously from the Middle East. "Where are you from?" I asked.

"Iran," he answered.

"Are there many Christians in Iran?"

"I never met one," he replied.

"So why do you have a cross hanging from your mirror?"

Then he told his story. "I was an army officer when the Shah was overthrown and the Ayatollahs came to power. They preached a harsh religion of intolerance and hate, and it made me hate religion. I left Iran, and I vowed never to set foot in a mosque again. After years in the States, a neighbor invited me to his church. I decided to go, to find out if what I learned about Christianity was true. That Sunday, I heard about a God of love, a God of mercy, a God who tells us to call him 'Father' and who sent his son to die for us. This message moved me very deeply. So I kept going back, and I became a Christian."

This Lent let's lift our heads and look around—at the family, the neighborhood, the workplace. Who needs to experience the love of God? Pray and fast for them. Reach out to them. Listen to their story. Invite them to your home for a cup of coffee, a glass of wine, or a meal. Invite them to your church home for Mass or a Lenten mission. If they are not Catholic, invite them to see what a Catholic church is like. No pressure. If they've been away, invite them to see what your parish is like. Next time you are going to confession, invite someone to come with you.

The Iranian cabdriver could have said no. But he had a right to know the truth about his heavenly Father. And his neighbor had a duty to introduce him. Thank God that his neighbor's love was greater than his fear of getting a "no."

Now there's a good thing to give up for Lent—the fear of rejection!

FOURTH SUNDAY OF LENT

Grace

As the camera pans the crowd at a football game, you see a few fans holding up the sign. It simply says "John 3:16."

For years, evangelical Protestants have extolled this little Bible verse as the heart of the Gospel. In their minds, if you only have a moment to tell people something about the Christian faith, this is the Scripture to quote: "For God so loved the world that he sent his only Son that whosoever believes in him may not die but may have eternal life."

Pope Paul VI, in his landmark letter on evangelization, confirmed that this verse is indeed is the central theme of the entire Bible.

So now comes the million-dollar question: How could a loving God ever send anyone to hell?

The answer is very simple. He doesn't.

Oh, hell certainly exists, all right. We see its crowded waiting room here on earth and can, if we observe closely, get some insight as to why its occupants are sitting there.

War certainly comes close to being hell on earth, especially when you happen to be on the losing side. Armed conflict is always nasty. But in the ancient world, despite the low level of technology, war was often total. When a city resisted a conquering army, it was made an example to neighboring towns. Jerusalem, for example, was razed to the ground by the Babylonians. The pride and joy of Israel, Solomon's temple, was reduced to a heap of rubble, civilians as well as soldiers put to the sword, and a few lucky ones led into exile.

Did God bring this hellish fate upon them? Not in the least. He actually sent messengers to tell them how to prevent such a tragedy. Jeremiah warned Jerusalem to repent and offer no resistance to the invaders. Their response? They imprisoned him. Through stubborn and foolish arrogance, they brought their fate crashing down upon their own heads, much to God's dismay.

Eternal punishment comes in exactly the same way. None are in hell except those who choose to be. "And this is the judgment, that the light has come into the world, and men loved darkness rather than light, because their deeds were evil" (John 3:19). Why would anyone walk away from the light? Perhaps because they don't like what they see as they emerge from the shadows. Maybe because they don't want anyone else to see them as they really are. They'd rather keep up the charade that they are good people and can fend for themselves, thank you very much. They've always done what's right and deserve to be appreciated, even applauded, by God and everyone else.

At the moment of death, the choice for light or darkness becomes final and irrevocable. But before that time, God is waiting for us to turn to him. He is rich in mercy (see Ephesians 2:4). He shines his light on our sins and brokenness not to humiliate us, but to irradiate the vermin that infects us and to clear up our blotchy complexions. All we need is the courage to face the truth about ourselves and rejoice in his merciful love that accepts us no matter what we've done or who we are. All we need is to be willing to say "sorry" and "thanks." For we can do nothing to earn his favor—it comes to us as a pure, undeserved gift (see Ephesians 2:4).

But God can't give us his mercy if we don't ask for it. And if we insist on "pulling our own weight," and getting from God what's coming to us, he'll do as we request. Jesus offers us a share in what he deserves from our heavenly Father. I think I'd opt for that rather than what I deserve!

Lent is a time to remember that we live by the mercy of God and to renew our determination that the grace that he has so generously lavished upon us will not be received in vain.

DAY 23

Reach out to the least important, least popular, most ignored person in your school, job environment, neighborhood, or whatever social group you find yourself in. Express a sincere interest in that person by smiling and asking questions about that person's interests, family, and well-being. Then listen.

"Nice guys finish last," says the world.

"The last will be first," replies Jesus.

My guess is that the Lord of creation knows best who really wins in the end. And he says this: "For every one who exalts himself will be humbled, and he who humbles himself will be exalted" (Luke 14:11).

To understand why the humble get ahead and why the meek will inherit the earth, we need to be sure that we understand what humility and meekness really are.

Humility does not mean looking down on oneself or thinking ill of oneself. It really means not thinking of oneself very much at all.

The humble are free to forget themselves because they are secure. They accept the fact that, as creatures, they are small, vulnerable, and not ultimately in control. But they know there is a Creator who is great, omnipotent, and totally in control. And they know that they've been made in the image and likeness of that Creator. That gives them a dignity they don't have to earn and can never be taken away. Though they've tarnished the divine likeness through sin, they know that the Creator came down from the heights of heaven to become human and fix what they couldn't fix.

So when they mess up, the humble don't have to cover up. They just say, "Please forgive me," give thanks for God's mercy, and move on. And when their creaturely limitations cause them to fail, they are not surprised. They realize that they are not God.

All this is simply a way of saying that the humble are in touch with reality. If the definition of insanity is being out of touch with reality, then our proud world with its "nice guys finish last" illusion is clearly insane.

Since the humble are secure, they are strong. And since they have nothing to prove, they don't have to flaunt their strength or use it to dominate others. Humility leads to meekness. And meekness is not weakness. Rather, it is strength under control, power used to build up rather than tear down.

The humble are not threatened either by God's greatness or the reflection of that greatness in the talents of others. In fact, this is what naturally catches their eye and absorbs their attention—the goodness of God, wherever it may be found.

The form of prayer that extols God's goodness is called praise. The activity that honors God's goodness in other people is called affirmation. The humble take delight in praising God and affirming people.

The reason the humble take the last place of honor at the table is not because they think ill of themselves, but because they are preoccupied with honoring others. And the reason people ask them to move higher is because they know this admirable attitude to be rare. In fact, it is actually divine. It is exactly the way the three Divine Persons relate to each other. The Father glorifies the Son, the Son glorifies the Father, and the Spirit is so preoccupied with glorifying the Father and the Son that most of us feel we really don't know much about him.

"An attentive ear is the wise man's desire" (Sirach 3:29). The humble are able to truly listen to another with genuine interest and delight in the other's goodness. The humble are the people who give you their undivided attention and make you feel special and appreciated. You love to have them around. You love to work hard for them. You cheer when they are honored.

The proud, on the other hand, are so self-absorbed that their conversations become monologues. When you are speaking, they are not listening. They're just thinking about what they are going to say next. Eventually you smile, yawn, and do your best to get away from them. You roll your eyes when they brag of their exploits. If you work for them, you do the minimum required while looking for a better job. So those who exalt themselves are ultimately left alone. But those who humble themselves gather a crowd of admirers.

When asked to name the four cardinal virtues, St. Bernard of Clairvaux replied, "Humility, humility, humility, and humility." He said this because the word *cardinal* means "hinge." And everything hinges on humility. Humility opens the door to the hearts of others and to the heart of God.

DAY 24

Read a biography of a saint, such as the newly canonized Sts. John XXIII and John Paul II. If you are more of a listener than a reader, find an audiobook version. (See the suggestions in the Lenten Resources, on page 116.)

In 1958, a congenial old man, Angelo Roncalli, was elected to the chair of Peter. He was to be a caretaker pope, someone to keep the ship steady while the cardinals identified a more long-term leader. That smiling old man soon stunned the world by calling the first ecumenical council in nearly a hundred years. That was not exactly what the cardinals had in mind.

But they had chosen a profoundly holy man for the job, someone who would be canonized just a few decades later. One thing about holy people— they are docile to the Holy Spirit. The Spirit blows where he wills, and they follow without hesitation. Don't choose that sort of person to man the helm if you don't want to rock the boat. Docility requires humility, which is a critical component of holiness in any age. If there was a salient characteristic of Angelo Roncalli, it was humility.

Born to a peasant sharecropping family of Northern Italy, Angelo never lost touch with his roots. As a seminarian, he spent his summers working the fields with his brothers. Whenever he removed the white gloves of papal ceremonial, one could see the calloused hands of a peasant.

Pope John XXIII was the first pontiff to allow representatives of atheistic communist governments to visit the Vatican. On one occasion he received a Soviet diplomat and his wife in private audience. He handed the wife a gift, a beautiful rosary. When he placed the beads in her hand, she exclaimed to her husband in Russian, "Look, he has the hands of a worker; he is one of us!" Of course she did not expect this peasant-pope to understand. But she was wrong! This peasant spoke not only Latin and his native Italian, but also French, Greek, Bulgarian, Turkish, and Russian. Duty required that he learn them. Duty had also required that he become an expert in the Fathers of the Church and the Reformation, so he got his doctorate in Church history. A highly cultured peasant indeed!

Yet the comment of the Russian woman gave him great satisfaction—he was proud to be recognized as a peasant, a worker, "one of us."

That highlights another quality of John's holiness that is a model for us all. No one left his presence without feeling that they had something profoundly in common with him, that he was with them, that he was for them. Everyone, even atheists, felt somehow affirmed by him.

This is not to say that he was without principles. At the outset of the council, he strongly affirmed that the essence of Catholic doctrine and morals would not change to suit modern tastes. He had strong convictions about modesty in dress, and he frequently reminded those who forgot. In his opening speech, he included strong criticism of those "prophets of doom" who saw nothing but sin and danger in the modern age.

Yet he was always able to distinguish persons from their actions or ideas, and recognize the human dignity of everyone. His affirming smile let people know that he found something delightful in them, the goodness of God that could not be obscured by their sins or politics. He was always able quickly to find some common ground and build rapport.

He was not liberal or conservative. He was just Angelo Roncalli, disciple and priest of Jesus Christ. The conservatives loved him because of his traditional piety. The liberals claimed him because he was open to change.

Yet there was not a political bone in his body. He was not trying to be "diplomatic." He was just transparently himself. Always. This is why he was chosen to serve in the Vatican diplomatic core for so many years. Because of his authenticity and integrity, everyone trusted him. He succeeded where others failed, building bridges, reconciling foes, defusing crises. Few know that when the Cuban missile crisis brought the world to the brink of nuclear war, it was Pope John who helped Kennedy and Khrushchev come to a peaceful resolution.

Pope John's ability to get erstwhile enemies talking was part of why the Holy Spirit was able to use him to make Vatican II happen. He made progressives and traditionalists sit down at the same table and work together. When some wished to submit their resignations, he refused with a smile and told them it was their duty to listen to each other and collaborate for the glory of God.

Saint that he was, he took God's work and God's glory very seriously. Yet his holiness prevented him from taking himself and his glory too seriously. He had the proverbial "Roman nose," big ears, and a waistline reflecting his love of pasta. When he was given a glimpse of himself for the first time in a full-length mirror, dressed in full papal regalia, his secretary overheard him mutter under his breath with a smile, "My God, this pope is going to be a disaster on television!"

DAY 25

Begin or widen the practice of praying a family rosary. If starting with once a week, try Friday or Sunday. If it's tough to start with a full five decades, start with just one. Try using a resource such as the Scriptural Rosary and have a different person read each of the Scriptures between the Hail Marys. This gets everyone more involved. As you pray, imagine Mary pondering the mysteries of faith with you and praying for you to grow in faith.

The Beatitudes rank high on the list of all-time favorite Bible passages. But what is a beatitude, anyway? In the Bible, a "blessed" person is someone who has received gifts of the greatest value, gifts that lead to true fulfillment and lasting happiness.

If I were to ask you to name the first beatitude, you'd probably say, "Blessed are the poor in Spirit." According to Matthew, you'd be right—but not according to Luke. At the very beginning of his Gospel, Luke reveals that the very first beatitude is uttered by a woman filled with the Spirit, speaking of another woman overshadowed by the Spirit. Elizabeth said of her cousin Mary, "Blessed is she who believed" (Luke 1:45).

Is Marian devotion important in Christian life? This has been a bone of contention between Catholics and Protestants for nearly five hundred years.

Let's look at the evidence in just the first chapter of Luke. First, the Angel Gabriel honors Mary with the greeting, "Hail, full of grace" (Luke 1:28). Then Elizabeth prophesies, "Blessed are you among women." Next the prophet John leaps for joy in his mother's womb at the sound of Mary's voice. Then, in her response to Elizabeth, Mary prophesies, "All generations will call me blessed" (Luke 1:48).

But it is Elizabeth's final words to Mary that hold the key to understanding why she is to be honored—namely, for her faith.

One of the battle cries of the Protestant Reformation was "Faith Alone!" A key conviction that united the many disparate strands of the Reformation was that it is impossible to earn God's favor by our good works; rather, we receive his love as a pure gift, a grace, through faith.

Now consider Mary. Did she crisscross the Mediterranean planting churches like Paul? Did she give eloquent sermons like Stephen (Acts 7)? Did she govern the Church like Peter? No. Her claim to fame is that she simply said yes to God. She believed he could do as he said and would do as he said.

But true faith is not just an intellectual conviction that God exists or that he can do thus and such. Faith involves entrusting oneself, abandoning oneself to God, and being willing to submit to his will. That's why Paul talks about "the obedience of faith" (Romans 16:26). Mary surrendered her plan for her life and yielded to God's plan. And she did this not once, but again and again, even when Jesus left her to begin his public ministry. And when that ministry led to the horror of Calvary, her faith stood its ground at the foot of the cross.

Therefore, Catholics honor Mary for being the perfect example of the greatest Protestant virtue. Ironic, isn't it? And the deepest meaning of that disputed doctrine, the Immaculate Conception, is that it was the grace of God working mysteriously from the moment of conception that made possible Mary's exemplary life of faith. Even her faith is a gift of God's grace. It's all grace, according to Catholic doctrine.

Mary, of course, knew this. That's why she responded to Elizabeth's praise with the humble, exuberant prayer known as the Magnificat: "My soul magnifies the Lord, and my spirit rejoices in God my Savior" (Luke 1:46–47). She is like the crystal-clear pool that reflects the sun's rays back to the heavens. No one needs to fear that honor given her will detract from the majesty of her divine Son. She deflects all the praise given her right back to God, the source of her greatness.

So the answer is that Marian devotion is necessary in Christian life. But what is true devotion to Mary according to the fathers of the Second Vatican Council? Not sentimental piety or gullible preoccupation with every rumored apparition, but imitation of her virtues, particularly her faith (see *Lumen Gentium*, 67).

DAY 26

Make it a daily practice to pray for the Holy Father's intentions, which are truly universal, and also for at least one special need beyond the frontiers of your native land. Look for an organization through which you can make a contribution to meet this need.

Most religions in the ancient world were local, national cults. The Egyptians worshiped Isis and Osiris. Athens was named after the goddess Athena. Ephesus was the center of the cult of Artemis.

But when the Church was born on Pentecost Sunday, it was comprised of people of every nation under heaven who each heard the good news in their own native tongue (see Acts 2). God's plan had always been for humanity to be one family. Sin had divided and scattered us (see Genesis 11), but now, in a reverse of the Tower of Babel, the many tongues of the human race become a sign of unity instead of alienation. Christ had died for all and, in the Great Commission (see Matthew 28:19), had sent his apostles to all. And so his Church was not to be a sect for the chosen few, but for "every nation, from all tribes and peoples and tongues" (Revelation 7:9). That's why at least from the beginning of the second century, the Church was called "catholic," from the Greek word meaning "according to," or "for the whole." The Catholic Church makes the "whole" treasury of Christ available to the "whole" world.

But don't we have special responsibilities to our own family, community, and nation? Absolutely. We can't save the world while our family and neighborhood go to pot. In fact, anyone who neglects to provide for the needs of the family "has disowned the faith and is worse than an unbeliever" (1 Timothy 5:8). And according to the teaching of St. Thomas Aquinas and others, we have a special, patriotic duty toward our own nation from which we've received so much.

Yet truly Catholic charity cannot stop here. The boundaries of our hearts must be stretched beyond our own families and national borders. True, our hearts are not quite as infinite as the heart of God. Our time, energy, and financial resources are limited. But every Catholic individual and family who wishes to be worthy of the name must find some regular way to universalize the work of mercy, however modest this way may be.

Lent is a special time to examine and stretch our hearts even as we tighten our belts. Curtailing some of our secular entertainment frees up time to learn about international needs and time to pray and even work to meet those needs. Fasting from "extras" during this season can also free up funds for the needy of the world.

We don't have to look too far to become aware of glaring needs. The news media, social media, and the Internet bring the suffering of the world into our living rooms and onto our mobile phones. The ravages of persecution and war in the Middle East and Africa require intense and immediate attention. China may be moving towards capitalism, but it is still far from democracy: There are hundreds of thousands of Chinese in slave labor camps, many of them Catholics and Protestants guilty of worshiping in a Church unapproved by the state. In some Muslim countries, the government looks the other way when fanatical mobs vandalize Churches and terrorize the Christian minority.

So what can we do about all this?

Pray: Intercession is one of the spiritual works of mercy. The pattern for our personal and family prayer is set by the Church's liturgy. Notice that the prayer of the faithful is also called the Universal Prayer since it is supposed to bring before God our Father the needs of the Church and the human family throughout the world. Make it a daily practice to pray for the Holy Father's intentions, which are truly universal, and also at least one particular need beyond the frontiers of your native land.

Help persecuted Christians: Christians throughout the world are still being persecuted and even martyred for their faith on a daily basis. Since the secular news media is usually oblivious to this, you have to work a bit to learn what is really going on. The Voice of the Martyrs and the Jubilee Campaign are two great organizations that provide this information, collect funds for the families of those in prison, and organize publicity campaigns that can be very effective in obtaining release or improved treatment of Christian prisoners. At times, these organizations even provide addresses of imprisoned Christians, making it possible for us to send them letters of prayer and support. Such letter writing campaigns are great projects for families and Catholic schools.

Feed the poor: Some of the money we save from Lenten sacrifices can be sent to an organization—Catholic or secular—that is especially efficient in providing food, clothing, shelter, and employment opportunities to the poor of impoverished countries. Two of my favorites are Catholic Relief Services and Food for the Poor.

Help missionaries: Billions of people on this planet have never heard the gospel of our Lord Jesus Christ. Many people falsely conclude that, since Vatican II teaches that it is possible for those who don't hear the Gospel to be saved, foreign missions are no longer necessary. Vatican II, to the contrary, said that foreign mission work is more urgent today than ever. Following the Second Vatican Council, Pope Paul VI wrote a moving encyclical on evangelization in the modern world, emphasizing once again the need to preach the gospel to all nations. Foreign missionaries need our prayers and financial support.

Make it personal: When we began our family, my wife and I wanted to find a way to create a more meaningful bond between our family and someone in need in the third world. So we decided to sponsor a needy child from Chile through a Catholic organization called the Christian Foundation for Children and Aging. We received regular letters and photos from this sponsored child, who is now an adult. Our children could read his letters and write back. Our modest monthly contribution and occasional Christmas and birthday gifts had much greater buying power in Chile, providing a Catholic education plus food and shelter for this young man. It meant a lot to watch the great difference we were able to make in one person's life.

Welcome immigrants: In the Old Testament, the Lord God of Israel had a special bond with those in Israelite society who had no one to depend upon but him: the widow, the orphan, and the stranger (or immigrant). The Israelites were once strangers in a strange land, far from homeland and family, and so they were commanded to take special care of immigrants in their midst. There is always a tendency for successive generations to forget the immigrant status of their forebears and become indifferent or even hostile to new immigrant groups. This happened in ancient Israel, and it happens in America today. We can demonstrate Catholic, universal charity right in our own communities by welcoming families moving to our area from other nations and cultures.

It's true that many of us struggle to make ends meet at times. But we have to keep in mind that in comparison with a majority of the world's population, even the poor among us are rich. The daily earnings of a minimum wage worker in the United States are more than the average monthly income of a worker in Haiti.

From those to whom much has been given, much will be expected. While none of us can singlehandedly ease all the world's suffering, all of us can certainly do something. Lent is a time to stop for a moment and ask how—within the boundaries of our duties and budget—we can extend the reach of our love.

DAY 27

Meditate on the Lord's passion every Friday. Make the Stations of the Cross or pray the sorrowful mysteries of the rosary, either alone or, better yet, with others, especially your family.

Catholics seem preoccupied with the sufferings of Christ—the crucifix, the sorrowful mysteries, the Stations of the Cross. As if all this were not enough, Catholics must stand at attention one Sunday each year as they listen to the entire Passion narrative read aloud.

Careful, repeated meditation on the passion of Christ is important because the passion is the climax of the entire history of revelation and redemption. It is the ultimate revelation of two intertwined realities: human sin and divine love.

First, let's talk about sin. People often think of sin merely as a transgression of God's arbitrary law, as a blot on our heavenly driving record. Meditation on Christ's passion makes us know better. Sin not only alienates us from God, it corrupts us, debases us, and enslaves us. The fickle crowd that carpets Christ's way into Jerusalem with palms drives him out a few days later with a cross on his back. One of his own betrays him to his enemies; another denies him. The Roman soldiers, to whom he did no wrong and was no threat, took diabolical pleasure in brutalizing him. Hard to believe that human beings are capable of such cruelty. Auschwitz reminds us that such evil really does lurk in the hearts of men. Then there is Pilate, who seems to be a much more reasonable figure. Maybe he is more like us. He just wants to keep the peace, preserve his relationship with the Jewish leaders and the emperor. If it means allowing an innocent man to be tortured to death—well, it's regrettable, but that's the price of living in the real world. Ultimately, Pilate's sin is an act of cowardice. Remember, sin is not just *commission* but *omission*. It involves what we do and what we fail to do, as we say in the Confiteor.

But, you say, it had to be so. God planned it this way. It was all predicted in the Scriptures. Yes, but God's foreknowledge does not mean he predetermined it. All the actors in the drama were free and responsible. Their sins are our sins. Indeed, they represent all of us, Jew and Gentile, male and female, black, white, and yellow. That's why Mel Gibson made an appearance in *The Passion of the Christ*—it was his hands that held down Jesus's hands as they were nailed to the cross.

But the story of the passion is even more importantly a revelation of who God is. First John 4:8 says that God is love. The passion shows us what love means. Love cannot sit idly by in the face of suffering. It instead leaves comfort behind and risks itself to mount a rescue mission. Love, therefore, must first empty himself of glory at the Father's right hand and take the form of a slave (see Philippians 2:6–11)—from the splendor of heavenly glory to the squalor of a stinking stable. As if that were not enough, Love surrenders himself into the hands of those who torture him to death. He saw their torches coming in the valley as he prayed in the Garden. He could have walked over the mountain and disappeared without a trace in the Judean wilderness. Or he could have used his divine power at any moment to scatter the temple guard and the Romans. Until the very end, he could have come down from that cross, as the crowd taunted him to do.

But that's just it. He had to love until the very end (see John 13:1). He had to love without limit. The fullness of love in a human heart means a love that was absolutely unstoppable by anything that hell and fallen humanity could hurl against it. And no love, no commitment, is total unless it entails the supreme sacrifice of one's life.

That's what was necessary to redeem us out of slavery to evil, to get us out of Egypt and through the Red Sea, across the Jordan, and into the Promised Land. It was for our freedom that he died; let's not again willingly submit ourselves to the bondage of sin.

Visit someone confined to their home in your neighborhood, or someone in the hospital, in a nursing home, or in prison. Is there a widowed or divorced person in your neighborhood who lives alone? Invite this person to your home for dinner or coffee.

What will the Last Judgment be like? By what criteria will we be judged?

Only one passage in the Gospels provides a sneak preview of that day of reckoning—Matthew 25:31–46. First of all, note that most of Jesus's parables have a jarring punch line. He's always upsetting the preconceived notions of just about everyone, especially the most religious of the bunch, whether they be Pharisees or disciples.

Clearly, all of us expect that the judge will condemn evil and impose a sentence on the guilty. And we tend to think of evildoing as stepping over the line and infringing on the rights of others, taking their possessions, maybe even taking their lives. The language of the Our Father lends itself to this interpretation of sin when it says, "Forgive us our trespasses."

The problem with this understanding of sin is that it is incomplete, even shallow. Lots of people think that as long as they don't lie, cheat, and steal, but just keep to themselves and mind their own business, they deserve big rewards from God.

The story of the Last Judgment addresses these "decent folks." Imagine their shock as they swagger smugly up to the judge's bench expecting praise only to be sent off to eternal punishment! Why? Because they neglected to do the good that love required them to do. They did not "commit" offenses or infractions of the law; they did nothing positively destructive. It's just that, in the presence of suffering, they heartlessly did absolutely nothing. Their sin was not a sin of commission but a sin of omission. But note: These sins of omission ultimately seal the fate of the damned.

There are lots of negative commandments, often expressed as "thou shalt nots." But the two most important commandments are positive "thou shalts."

"You shall love the Lord, your God, with all your heart, with all your soul, and with all your strength" and "You shall love your neighbor as yourself" (Matthew 22:37, 39). These commandments require an interior disposition that naturally produces outward actions. If you are hungry, you love yourself enough to go to the fridge or drive to McDonald's. If you truly love your hungry neighbor as yourself, you don't just say a prayer and offer sympathy (see James 2:15–17). Loving God with all your heart doesn't mean giving a respectful nod to God and then going on your merry way. It means going *out* of your way, passionately seeking to love your neighbor and serve him in all you do.

In this Last Judgment scene, we see how these two commandments are really one. Jesus makes clear that loving God with your whole heart is expressed in loving your neighbor as yourself. And whenever you love your neighbor in this way, you are actually loving the Son of God.

So ultimately, the judgment is simple. It all comes down to love. The judge happens to be the King of hearts.

FIFTH SUNDAY OF LENT

Lazarus

Some find it hard to accept that God would love some people more than others. That wouldn't be fair, they say.

But God became man. If he did not love some more than others, Jesus wouldn't be fully human. For human beings have family and friends. While we can do good and even risk our lives for a stranger, we have special bonds of intimacy and affection with a rather small circle. Out of twelve, Jesus had one especially beloved. In the Gospel of this beloved disciple, we learn that Jesus had one family who was particularly beloved in this way. The family was that of Mary, Martha, and their brother Lazarus.

So it was amazing to all that Jesus did not come immediately when he heard that Lazarus was ill (John 11:1–45). Of course he was a busy man. But Jesus had dropped everything many times before to heal strangers. This, on the other hand, was one of his dearest friends. Not to worry, he explained to his disciples. This sickness would not end in death.

So imagine their surprise when he tells them a few days later that Lazarus was dead and they were going to visit the grave. Jesus knew what he was going to do. Yet when he was met by a distraught Mary and her weeping companions, he did not rebuke them for crying. He did not say they should wear white and rejoice that their brother had finally gone home to heaven. No, he wept with them.

Some people accept death as a natural part of human life. Others think that death is merely a portal to eternity. Jesus saw death as an enemy. His Father had never intended for us to experience it. In fact, he forbade Adam and Eve only one thing—a fruit that would make them subject to it. It was through the envy of the devil that death came into the world, not the plan of God. Death wrenches the soul from the body. It rips loved ones from the embrace of their families. So in the presence of those wounded by death's sting, Jesus weeps.

Jesus's miracles in the Gospels always spring from his compassion for the suffering. But he always has more in mind than just helping the victim lying before him. His miraculous works in John's Gospel are called signs because they point beyond themselves to something still greater he will do to gain an even greater benefit for all.

This is why Jesus allowed Lazarus to die in the first place. In calling him forth from the tomb, Jesus was making clear why he had come. His teaching was, of course, sublime, and his cures were life-changing. But wiser and healthier people still faced the horror of death. If Jesus were really the Savior, he had to save us from the grave. And the salvation would have to be a permanent one. Lazarus's resuscitation was only a stay of execution. A few years later, the mourners would have to assemble around his bedside once again.

So in the presence of the great crowd who had assembled for the funeral, Jesus called Lazarus out of the tomb. This demonstration of Jesus's power over death was a sign of his own coming resurrection—and of Lazarus's and ours as well.

This is the last recorded miracle or "sign" in John's Gospel. Jesus knew it would be. You and I might expect that the news of this miracle, brought back to Jerusalem by numerous eyewitnesses, would lead to the acceptance of Jesus as Lord and Messiah. But the Lord knew it would have the exact opposite effect. It demonstrated to his enemies just how great a threat he was. They had to act fast to stop this sort of thing from getting out of hand.

But that was all part of his plan. For Jesus was in control. He planned to lay his life down willingly, to experience the horrible torture of crucifixion, the bitter wrenching of body from soul and friend from friend. He was willing to do this because, by means of it, he knew he would accomplish more for us than he had for Lazarus—a victory over death that would last forever.

DAY 29

Commit to making an examination of conscience each night before bed, reviewing the thoughts, words, and actions of your day to see if all were motivated by love of God. Ask forgiveness where you fell short.

In his space trilogy, C.S. Lewis called him "the Bent One." That is really an apt name for the one the Bible is calls "Satan" or the Accuser. The perverse choice he made to serve himself rather than his creator warped his nature, and ever since he has taken delight in twisting anything he can get his hands on.

Take sexual desire, for instance. It was created by God to draw a man and woman together in committed, covenant love that issues in new life. As such, sexual desire is clearly a great good. But when it is twisted at the instigation of "the Bent One," it becomes lust—the urge for sterile self-gratification that is willing to trample upon the dignity of another, or many others, to satisfy an itch.

The same holds true for economic drive. Nowhere in the Bible do we see praise for laziness or indigence. Man and woman are given responsibility to care for the garden even before sin enters into the story. Work is holy, and it ought to be productive (St. John Paul II's theology of work is as fantastic as his theology of the body). And enjoying the fruit of our labor, as well as sharing it with others, are some of the greatest blessings of human life.

Yet, when the drive to work and earn money is twisted, the legitimate pleasure intended by God vanishes, and bondage ensues. The workaholic can't get off the treadmill to enjoy the fruit of his labor. He anxiously allows work to become compulsive, eating away at every area of his life. Then we have the greedy of this world who hoard their treasure, unable to enjoy it themselves or share it with others. Instead, money becomes a substitute for God (that, by the way, is the definition of an idol). The greedy seek their identity and ultimate security in money. This is what we see in the rich man of Luke 12:13–21. His problem is not that he is excited about a bumper harvest, but that he succumbs to the illusion that this wealth means security. He puts his trust in his warehouses, and of course, they let him down.

We learn in 1 Timothy 6:10 that the love of money is the root of all evil. I've always found St. Augustine's definition of the love of money to be very enlightening. He points out that the wrong kind of love is not restricted to money. Whenever a created thing becomes no longer a means to love God, but an end in itself, you have a "love" that is idolatry. Do you "love" the idea of finding the perfect mate? To have a better love life within marriage? To have a child? To get a job? To win an athletic championship? To get a college degree? To flourish in business? The desire for all these things can be good indeed. The avid pursuit of each of these things can actually be a duty, depending on one's state in life.

The question, though, is whether these desires and achievements are stepping-stones on the road to God or disastrous detours. We need to get honest with ourselves. Are we most intent on things below or on things above? (see Colossians 3:2). We should be passionate about many things below—but is our zeal for health, love, kids, education, a job, and financial security truly a function of our zeal for loving God and doing his will? Where do we seek our ultimate satisfaction and security? In these temporal things (even people) that pass away, or in God who is forever? What do we look forward to more—our next promotion or heaven? The great Catholic tradition of a nightly examination of conscience helps us ask such questions regularly and keeps us from getting off track.

If you haven't noticed, it does not take much to knock us off track. It's been that way ever since that fateful conversation in the Garden between our first parents and the Bent One.

Make a pilgrimage during Lent, or makes plans to do so in the near future. It could be a short journey that involves little to no expense, like to your diocesan cathedral or to a monastery or shrine within driving distance. Or it could be to Rome, Fatima, or the Holy Land.

Salvation history is the story of a journey. Abram goes from civilization to the desert, Moses from the Pharaoh's palace to a mountaintop. The people of Israel repeat Moses's journey and then are led through the desert to the Promised Land.

All these journeys have a few things in common. God inspired each of them and accompanied the travelers on their way. Through the journey, he changed them. At the destination, he blessed them.

When Israel finally settled in the land, God wanted to constantly remind them that they are perpetual pilgrims in this world and that he, not the land, is their true inheritance. So the Lord made Jerusalem the seat of his special presence on earth and commanded them to journey there three times a year to worship him with feasts of thanksgiving, such as the Passover. The public ministry of Jesus takes place against the background of these pilgrimages. Finally the already Holy City became even holier, sanctified forever by Christ's blood.

When Constantine became emperor in A.D. 312, the first priority was to decree religious freedom. But the next priority was to send his mother on pilgrimage to the Holy Land, where she had churches built that are still visited by pilgrims today. Next Constantine built churches in Rome over the tombs of Sts. Peter and Paul to welcome the pilgrims from all over the empire who would come to honor these two apostles of the Lamb.

Ever since, Christians have braved all sorts of difficulties and road hazards to visit Jerusalem, Rome, the sites of Marian apparitions, and the homes of saints. They have come not as tourists, but as pilgrims. There is a difference! A pilgrimage is not primarily a vacation. The ultimate goal is not recreation, but re-creation. It is a journey of devotion, undertaken by the prompting of the Holy Spirit. The purpose? To worship God, do penance, and be transformed. Pilgrimage to a holy place is so spiritually powerful that, under the Old Covenant, it was required. Though not required today, it is so highly recommended that the Church offers a plenary indulgence to all those who answer the call.

I was a college student when I was first invited to make a Holy Year pilgrimage to Rome. Initially I brushed off this suggestion as ridiculous. I was broke, like most college students. Besides, the pilgrimage took place during final exams. But I felt an inner tug that I thought just might be the Holy Spirit. I had been struggling with a holier-than-thou attitude that I simply could not overcome. I had been pleading with God to help me. Maybe, I thought, this pilgrimage was his answer to my prayer. So I spoke to my professors. They gladly rescheduled my exams. I began cobbling money together. Soon there was enough. I decided to go and make the trip as a penitential pilgrimage, seeking the grace to change.

It was an amazing adventure. The experience of Rome bonded me to the Catholic Church, its heritage, and its rich tradition, in a very profound way. It whetted my appetite for learning. Some friendships were deepened, and many new friends made. But the most important thing was a gift of special grace that I received when I least expected it. Very early one morning, before St. Peter's was filled with tourists, I spent some quiet moments roaming through the crypt. I felt moved to kneel down to pray at one of the tombs, and there I received a touch of God that I will never forget. The tomb was that of John XXIII (now a saint), who had a remarkable gift of humility and a unique ability to make people feel loved, affirmed, and appreciated. These gifts were exactly what I lacked and for which I had been praying. Some measure of his spirit was shared with me that day, and I was changed. The following year was among the happiest of my life.

I've since led nearly eight hundred people on pilgrimage to Rome and the Holy Land. I've seen countless miracles, even physical healings. As pilgrimage director, I am responsible for a million practical details. As you might imagine, this is quite a distraction! Nevertheless, there is always a special moment when God touches me in a very deep and new way, and I go from pilgrimage director to pilgrim.

The Holy Land brings Scripture alive. After going there, you'll never read the Bible the same way again. Rome knits you to the universal Church and the heritage of the saints in a way that's hard to describe. The medieval charm of Assisi, the beauty of Lourdes at the foot of the Pyrenees Mountains— these special places impart an atmosphere of serenity and draw one to deeper prayer.

But pilgrimage is about more than the place; it's about the grace. A special grace, custom-designed for each pilgrim by the Holy Spirit, imparted in God's perfect time. This is the greatest reason to listen for and respond to God's call to pilgrimage.

DAY 31

Before work, chores, or study, make a conscious decision to offer up whatever you are doing for the love of God and in loving intercession for some person or special need. Each Sunday, as the gifts are brought up to the altar, mentally place all these things on the paten with the altar bread.

At age sixteen, I thought that aspiring to holiness was out of the question. If you really wanted to be holy, I thought, you had to be a priest, nun, or brother. You had to spend your days doing "religious stuff" like praying, preaching, teaching catechism, or serving the poor. But I had developed an interest in the opposite sex and was headed toward a career in music, so I was disqualified. The best I could hope for was to avoid breaking the Ten Commandments, get to confession when I failed, not miss Mass on Sunday, and toss a few bucks in the collection each week. That way, I could at least make it to heaven after a stay in purgatory. But true sanctity? That was out of my reach.

If holiness were about marital status or what you do for a living, I would have been right. But the Second Vatican Council made very clear that my assumptions were wrong. Holiness is not about what you do, but with how much love you do it. Holiness is really the perfection of faith, hope, and sharing in God's very nature, which is love (see 1 John 4:8). We are talking about a special kind of love here, the love that gives freely of itself to another, that even lays down its own priorities, interests, and very life for another.

So is holiness difficult to attain? No. It is impossible—at least on our own steam. But that's the thrill of it all. God invites us into an intimate relationship with himself through Jesus. He takes up residence within us and makes it possible to love with his love. Grace is the love of God that comes into our hearts as a free, undeserved gift and enables us to be like God.

So does that mean spending all our time in the chapel? No—it means doing ordinary things with extraordinary love. The Virgin Mary, our greatest example of holiness, was a housewife and a mother. Jesus and his foster father, St. Joseph, apparently spent most of their lives doing manual labor. But when

Mary did the wash, she did it for love. When Joseph made a table, he did it for love. When hardship and danger threatened, they met it with faith, hope, and love.

Holiness is for every baptized person, regardless of personality type, career, age, race, or marital status. In baptism, we are all reborn with the spiritual muscles necessary to get us across the finish line. Yet these muscles must be nourished and exercised if they are ever to develop and carry us the full distance. God provides the necessary nourishment in the Word of God and the Eucharist. And he sends us ample opportunities to exercise.

But there's the rub—many of us don't want to exert ourselves. It can be uncomfortable. We stretch a bit to finish school, to excel at sports, to win the heart of the love of our lives. But when it comes to the things of the Spirit, we often settle with being couch potatoes.

Leon Bloy, a French Catholic writer, once said, "There is only one misfortune, not to be saints."* Holiness is about realizing our deepest, greatest potential, becoming who we were truly destined to be. What a shame it would be to miss it!

---

* Quoted in Jean Daujat, *The Faith Applied: Living Faith in Daily Life* (New York: Scepter, 2010), p. 98.

DAY 32

Pray regularly for those whose rights and dignity are trampled and for those responsible for their pain: crime victims and criminals, refugees, those touched by abortion, poverty, and human trafficking. Look for a way to help.

The various religions that existed in biblical times had gods who were made in man's image and likeness. The pagan gods had all the foibles and vices that can be viewed in a soap opera. They played favorites, schemed to destroy their enemies, cheated on their spouses, and held grudges.

The Bible proclaims that human beings are made in God's image and likeness. The God of the Bible is a community of persons who give themselves to each other eternally in love. This God of love is a sublime artist who creates the world as a masterpiece of beauty and nobility.

Sin gets in the way of all this, of course, defacing God's likeness in us. Every sin is an offense against God precisely because it debases us as well as others. But how does God respond to the outrage and ugliness of sin? He does not draw back in revulsion; instead, he draws near. He even assumes our human nature so he can come to our rescue. He never loses sight of the divine dignity hiding underneath the rags of our sin. He loves tax collectors Matthew and Zacchaeus right back into their dignity. He takes the time to listen to the Samaritan woman with five husbands and offers her a new life.

The Second Vatican Council draws out the implications of this biblical witness. It bases the right to freedom of religion on human dignity. It teaches that morality can never just be imposed from without as so many rules and regulations, but must be internalized in a sanctuary called conscience. It teaches that not just a select few but all are called to the heights of holiness, regardless of their state in life or occupation. It teaches that if all are created in God's image and likeness, then all are equal in dignity, whether man or woman, adult or child, born or unborn, cleric or lay. It teaches that we must work in society to bring about living conditions that correspond to human dignity.

The teaching of the Church is beautifully expressed in councils, encyclicals, and the *Catechism*. But it is expressed even more beautifully in the lives of its saints. The life of Blessed Teresa of Calcutta is a moving testimony to the dignity of the human person. Plunging into one of the world's most disgusting slums, she recognized and honored the image of God in people cast off by society and left to die in the gutter. Many would judge such creatures to be useless and revolting. She and her sisters loved them, befriended them, and stood with them till the end.

And then there is St. John Paul II, the apostle of human dignity. His opposition to the death penalty on grounds of human dignity caused quite a stir. But let's not forget how he himself responded when gravely wounded by an assassin. He did not simmer in resentment and outrage. Neither did he simply forget about the man. As the Good Shepherd went out after the lost sheep, the wounded pope went to the prison cell of his attacker, looked him in the eye, and spoke to him of forgiveness and God's love.

In raising these two witnesses to the dignity of the altar, the Church reaffirms the dignity of every single human person without exception.

Look for opportunities to volunteer for the lowliest, least-desirable jobs, and serve those who are least worthy and least grateful.

It was time to make their move. Usually it was Peter who took the initiative, but now it was their turn. They cleared their throats and asked the master for the best seats in the house, the places of honor right next to the throne.

Of course, in this conversation (see Mark 10:35–45), John and James were referring to that glorious moment when Jesus would be finally acclaimed king of Israel—indeed, of the whole world. They envisioned themselves as prime ministers "A" and "B" who should naturally bask in the splendor of the monarch.

Jesus was quite restrained in his correction. It was natural for the disciples to strive for excellence since God created us to do so. And it was natural for them to think that excellence meant privilege, honor, and glory, because that's how everyone seems to think of it, whether Jew or Gentile. Both chief priests and Roman governors were surrounded with pomp and circumstance, servants and sycophants.

Jesus wanted his disciples to be ambitious about achieving true greatness, which is having not big heads, but big hearts. It is that love called charity that makes men and women truly great, since it makes them like God, in whose image they were created. Jesus had begun to show his disciples what God's love was like, but they hadn't gotten the point. Their feet had not yet been washed, and their king had not been crowned with thorns. They had not yet understood that love is self-emptying, that true greatness lies in sacrifice, that "prime minister" means servant of all.

In a world where self-interest and self-promotion are the law of the land, such a love is destined to suffer. To be great in love is to suffer much. The cup of feasting may come, but only after the cup of suffering. Jesus had come to drain this bitter cup to its dregs. Were they ready to drink it with him? Glibly they answered yes, oblivious to the implications of their choice. They would learn soon enough what it would entail.

The Letter to the Hebrews says that Jesus can be compassionate and merciful with us because he was tempted in every way we are tempted, though he never succumbed (see Hebrews 4:14–16). He could correct the sons of Zebedee with gentleness because he himself was tempted to gain the favor and glory of the kingdoms of the world by bowing before the father of pride (see Matthew 4:8–9). He humbly chose instead to serve the Father of mercy.

You'd think it would be easier for us to get the point than those two brothers. After all, we received the spirit of understanding when, in baptism and confirmation, we put on the mind of Christ. We know the end of the story—that the resurrection follows the crucifixion.

But unfortunately, there's still a scar left on all us from the snakebite passed down to us by our first parents, and a residue of the serpent's venom still lingers. There is a tug within us to climb over others in our rise to greatness, to exalt ourselves at others' expense, even to trip up others so we can get ahead. We are tempted to let others take the rap so we might look good, to leave others holding the bag while we escape, to leave the dirty dishes for others lest, God forbid, we do more than our "fair share."

If we are to be followers of Jesus and achieve true greatness, we must renounce placing any limits on how much we are willing to give or whom we are willing to serve. The one who is greatest and most like God is not the one who appears on the cover of *People* magazine. It is the one who will go to the greatest lengths for those who are least worthy and least grateful.

DAY 34

Find out what the Sign of the Cross really means and begin making it less mechanically, more thoughtfully, several times per day.

To some, being Italian-American means overindulging in pasta and joking about tough guys. But being Italian also means being heir to a rich tradition stretching back before the Caesars. Included are philosophers such as Seneca, poets such as Dante, artists such as Michelangelo, and saints such as Francis of Assisi.

To some, being Catholic means giving up chocolate for Lent. But those who explore their Catholic heritage discover thousands of years of meaning, insight, and life-giving resources: inspiring stories about people from Abraham to Mother Teresa, practical instruction by some of the most brilliant thinkers of all time, and tried-and-true spiritual practices that make people grow in character and happiness.

In John 10:10, Jesus said, "I came that they may have life, and have it abundantly." That recalls Isaiah who, speaking of God's people, says: "Behold, I will extend prosperity to her like a river, / and the wealth of the nations like an overflowing stream" (Isaiah 66:12). The Catholic Church is all about preserving and enjoying the whole, rich heritage of Christ. In fact, the word *catholic* comes from the Greek word for "whole." The problem is that some preserve outward practices of this heritage, such as giving up something for Lent, but have lost the connection with the meaning and power of such customs and traditions.

Take, for example, the Sign of the Cross. For some it is just a mechanical part of "logging on" and "logging off" of our time "connected" to God via prayer. For others, it seems no more than a superstitious good-luck charm to employ before stepping up to bat.

To see what it really means, we need to examine where it comes from. In baptism, a cross is traced on the foreheads of the baptized. The same occurs in confirmation, when the tracing is done with sacred oil called "chrism." As the signing takes place, the name of the triune God is pronounced—Father, Son, and Holy Spirit.

How far back in time does this practice go? Paul says, "I bear on my body the marks of Jesus" (Galatians 6:17). Notice that in the book of Revelation, those doomed to death have the mark of the beast on their brow (14:11), while the 144,000 in white robes have been sealed on the forehead with the name of God and the Lamb (7:1–4). Sounds a lot like the Sign of the Cross, doesn't it?

In the early Church, the Sign of the Cross was seen as the brand mark on the body of a Christian indicating that he or she was now the property of a new master and under the protection of that master. The blood of the lamb on the doorposts of the Israelites protected them from the Angel of Death who "passed over" their homes. The Sign of the Cross on the Christian says, "Hands off!" to the powers of darkness. Note that Jesus says to his disciples, "I have given you authority to tread upon serpents and scorpions, and over all the power of the enemy; and nothing shall hurt you" (Luke 10:19). The Sign of the Cross is the sign of this authority.

But this sign means even more than belonging to the triune God. It indicates how and why we've come to belong to God and to be entitled to his protection. It means that for my standing with God, I do not trust in the good deeds that I've done or the "good person" that I am. Rather, I stake my claim to heaven on what Jesus did for me on Calvary. It means that I am saved by a pure gift of his love, by grace. "But far be it from me to glory except in the cross of our Lord Jesus Christ" (Galatians 6:14).

Each time I make this sign, it is a renewal of my "decision for Christ," my intimate relationship of love with the Father, Son, and Holy Spirit that comes as a pure gift of God's grace through faith, baptism, and confirmation. In this simple little sign is contained the very essence of the Gospel.

The good news is that everything in the Catholic heritage is like this—full of rich meaning that we've forgotten. But not to worry: We can recover the meaning and reactivate the power. Let's get busy exploring and unpacking the amazing Catholic tradition!

PALM SUNDAY

We now come to the Sunday with a split personality. It starts with an upbeat Gospel reading recounting Jesus's triumphal entry into Jerusalem. It is a festive affair, complete with a parade route strewn with palm branches instead of ticker tape. But we quickly progress to the stark reading of Jesus's passion, bearable only because we already know its happy ending. Mel Gibson's film *The Passion of the Christ* did us a favor in reminding us how shockingly brutal the whole business really was.

Two names for the same day: Palm Sunday and Passion Sunday. I propose a third name: Fickle Sunday. The same people who were cheering during the parade were jeering a few days later. They'd been wowed by Jesus's sermons, fed with loaves and fishes, healed of their diseases, and delivered of their demons. But as soon as the tide began to turn, so did they. Their cries of "Hosanna" turned to shouts of a very different kind: "Crucify him!"

Of course, Jesus was not surprised in the least. The Gospels tell us that he knew the human heart all too well. He was not fooled by all the acclamations and fanfare. Flattery could not swell his head. He had no illusions of grandeur or ambition for worldly glory. In fact, St. Paul tells us that he had willingly emptied himself of heavenly glory in pursuit of his true passion—his Father's will and our salvation (see Philippians 2:6–11).

He "set his face like flint" (see Isaiah 50:7) He was on a mission, and nothing would deter him. He barreled through barriers that usually stop us dead in our tracks—fear of ridicule, fear of suffering, abandonment by our closest companions. He was willing to endure the sting of sin to blot out sin, and he was eager to face death in order to overcome it.

He did indeed have a "well-trained tongue" (Isaiah 50:4). His words had mesmerized the crowds, intrigued Herod, and even made Pilate stop and think. But now his lips are strangely silent. All the Gospels point out that he said very little during his passion. They record only seven brief statements from the cross. Maybe this was to fulfill the Scripture that said, "Like a lamb that is led to the slaughter, / and like a sheep that before its shearers is silent, / so he opened not his mouth" (Isaiah 53:7). Actually, everything that happened in these fateful hours fulfilled Scripture. Isaiah 50 had foretold the beating and mockery. Psalm 22 lays it all out hundreds of years before it happens: his thirst, the piercing of his hands and feet by Gentiles (called "dogs" by the Jews), and the casting of lots for his clothing. The opening line of this psalm happens to be "My God, my God, why have you forsaken me?" Could it be that the Lord uttered this phrase to remind us that this was all in the plan?

So the virtual silence of his well-trained tongue fulfilled Scripture. But there was another reason for his silence. Though Jesus was destined to preach on Good Friday, the message was not to be delivered in words. The language of this sermon was to be body language. Good Friday, according to Jewish reckoning, actually began at sundown on Holy Thursday. On the beginning of his final day, Jesus gave us the verbal caption of his last and greatest sermon: "This is my body, which will be given for you.... This cup is the new covenant in my blood, which will be shed for you (Luke 22:19–20, *NAB*).

"I love you" is not so much something you say as it is something you demonstrate. Diamonds may be a moving testimony to love, but the laying down of one's life is even more compelling. And though this life is human and therefore vulnerable, it is also divine and therefore infinite in value—a gift so valuable that it outweighs every offense committed from the dawn of time until the end of the world. An act so powerful that it melts hearts, opens the barred gates of paradise, and makes all things new.

DAY 35

Learn the Prayer of Abandonment of Blessed Charles de Foucauld. Surrender your possessions, your future, and your life to God as you slowly pray it.

> *Father, I abandon myself into your hands;*
> *Do with me what you will.*
> *Whatever you may do, I thank you;*
> *I am ready for all, I accept all.*
> *Let only your will be done in me,*
> *and in all your creatures.*
> *I wish no more than this, O Lord.*
> *Into your hands I commend my soul;*
> *I offer it to you with all the love of my heart,*
> *for I love you, Lord, and so need to give myself,*
> *to surrender myself into your hands,*
> *without reserve and with boundless confidence,*
> *for you are my Father.*
> *Amen.* *

He was curious. He had already fulfilled all the elementary requirements. He was a decent person who hadn't killed anybody, had honored his parents, and would never think of stealing another man's goods or another man's spouse. But what would it take to advance beyond that to assurance of heaven, to perfection, to true intimacy with God?

Curiosity is not the same as desire. True desire will pay any price to get what it wants. Curiosity has the itch to know but not necessarily the will to act. Jesus decided to help this individual get honest with himself, for he saw the man's heart. After all, he is the Word of God made flesh, and Scripture says that God's word penetrates the surface and drives deep into a person, like a double-edged sword (see Hebrews 4:12). The gaze of the living Word

---

* Prayer of Abandonment of Blessed Charles de Foucauld, www.brothercharles.org/wordpress/prayer-of-abandonment/.

penetrates. And now he speaks words that also penetrate and even sting a bit. "Go, sell what you have, and give to the poor, and you will have treasure in heaven; and come, follow me" (Mark 10:21).

Immediately the man's countenance fell. He had not expected this sort of response. More prayers and fasting he could handle perhaps. But giving up all that he'd worked for? And traipsing after this itinerant rabbi all over who-knows-where, not knowing where his next meal would be coming from? It was all too much for him.

He wanted God as a part of his life. But he wasn't ready to give God control of his life, to abandon himself completely, to find his whole identity and security in the Lord. His affluence provided him with a level of comfort and prominence that he had learned to depend upon. It was just too scary to let go of that.

This was a crisis moment in his life, where a choice was set before him that would manifest where his heart truly lay. He tragically failed the heart monitor test.

But there was another young man, a thousand years earlier, who faced the same sort of test and responded differently (see Wisdom 7:7–11). His father had built a very nice kingdom for him. At the very point at which he was to take over the reins, the Word of God came to him and offered him anything he truly desired. What was his heart's desire? To be given riches surpassing the wealth of all other kings on the planet? To be granted stunning military victory over all his enemies?

Solomon chose neither of these. If he alone was in control of vast armies and riches, he could lose them in a heartbeat, or use them to do more harm than good. If he alone were calling the shots, trying to make himself and his people happy, he'd probably end up miserable and make his people miserable. Humility caused him to recognize his littleness and God's greatness. This respect for God's grandeur, otherwise known as fear of the Lord, is the beginning of wisdom. The first thing wisdom does is seek more wisdom. So that is what he asked for: God's wisdom, God's counsel, God's help, and even God's control. Ironically, putting the reins in God's hands enabled Solomon to bring military success and prosperity greater than Israel had ever enjoyed before or since.

Jesus points out how this works after the rich young man went away sad. Yes, those who give up precious relationships and possessions to follow Jesus will encounter hardship and persecution. But they will also receive, even in this life, infinitely more than they gave up and, in the age to come, everlasting life.

But God can't lead us on the adventure of a lifetime if we're still clinging desperately to what we think will make us happy, with the reins of our lives grasped tightly in our own hands.

DAY 36

Give thanks daily for your own cross—the trials and misfortunes in your life—with the confidence that God will turn them to good.

I once heard a successful CEO tell a diverse group of business leaders that, regardless of their religion, they simply had to read the Bible. Why? Because success in business depends not so much upon understanding financial reports as it does upon understanding people. And when it comes to a book that reveals what makes people tick, there is none better than the Bible.

Perhaps Christians ought to pay heed to this businessman. We often get our ideas about people more from our own wishful thinking than God's inspired Word. We expect that people will applaud and honor us when we live upright lives that are honorable, chaste, and charitable. We are shocked when they do the opposite.

Jesus wasn't. He knew that the miracles he performed to heal, feed, and deliver the poor, sick, and downtrodden, that the words he spoke which captivated them and gave them hope—all this might very well be perceived to be a blessing by many. But he knew that to some, it would be perceived as a threat.

For what the people so abundantly received from Jesus served to remind everyone of just how little they had received from their religious leaders. Both the book of Wisdom (2:12–20) and the Letter of James (3:16—4:3) describe the inner dynamic at work in the hearts of the wicked. When good people come across someone more virtuous, they are grateful. They are reminded of what they can become, and it encourages them to pursue excellence. They rejoice when the virtuous person is honored, and in fact they lead the applause. But when evil people come across someone more virtuous, they are furious. Such people serve as proof that the wicked could be different. The virtuous person takes away their excuses and exposes their mediocrity, so they resent his or her success. Rather than emulate the hero or heroine and strive to accomplish similar things, they instead seek to destroy the virtuous person and discredit his or her work, thereby removing the embarrassing threat to their own self-respect and image.

This goes beyond what we customarily mean by the term jealousy, for it is not simply wishing to possess a good thing enjoyed by another. Rather this sort of jealousy concludes, either through laziness or despair, that the good that it desires is impossible to attain and so aims to obliterate it and the person possessing it. It is the capital sin of envy, and it often employs ingenious strategies to bring down its nemesis.

Jesus understood all this. Amidst all the euphoria aroused by his sensational ministry, he predicted that he would be tortured to death at the instigation of the "spiritual" leaders of his own people.

But Wisdom incarnate had a plan much wiser than the clever schemes of his cunning opponents. Yes, they had it all worked out—he'd come to Jerusalem for the feast, as would the Roman procurator, the only one who could approve his execution. They'd recruit a snitch from his inner circle. They'd rig a kangaroo court, mustering the Sanhedrin in the middle of the night. They'd manipulate Pilate with fear of losing the emperor's favor.

But the worldly wisdom of envy was no match for the heavenly wisdom of Love. All their maneuvering only served to advance the purposes of God's own glorious plan of salvation. The elaborate machinations of evil men played right into Christ's hands, setting him up to win the eternal forgiveness of those who plotted against him.

For love, as St. Paul says in Romans 8:28, has the power to make everything work out for the good. And that is the reason that the crucifix is the central image of the Catholic faith. It is a symbol of faith, hope, and love. Yes, it demonstrates how much Christ loves us. But it also demonstrates that we have nothing to fear from the tragedies and calamities that have happened or could happen. Because if God can bring glory out of the shame of the cross, he can bring good out of anything.

DAY 37

Learn the Prayer of St. Ignatius. Pray it slowly, meaningfully, surrendering control of your life to the Lord.

> *Take, Lord, and receive all my liberty,*
> *my memory, my understanding,*
> *and my entire will,*
> *all I have and call my own.*
> *You have given all to me. To you, Lord, I return it.*
> *Everything is yours; do with it what you will.*
> *Give me only your love and your grace.*
> *That is enough for me.**

All of us want the very best for those we love. But as we pursue it, we often experience a rude awakening. The best turns out to be quite expensive, whether you are dealing with homes, cars, or colleges. To get it will cost much time and money, maybe even some blood, sweat, and tears.

We are then confronted with an important question. How badly do we really want the best? Is it a burning desire that is strong enough to propel us up the steep hill we need to climb to get to the top? Or would we rather just settle for less?

As Lent turns into Holy Week, the liturgical readings switch focus from our need for redemption to the dramatic choice looming before the Redeemer. He had leapt from heavenly glory to the indignity of a stable. He had left his mother for a band of uncomprehending disciples and a fickle crowd. That was all hard enough. But now, if he would fulfill the Father's plan to deliver us from the bondage of sin, even more would be required. Hebrews 5:7–9 speaks of Jesus's tears and loud cries to God, alluding to the agony in the garden. The Garden of Gethsemane, by the way, is on the slope of a mountain. The guards approaching the garden with their torches were visible to our Lord from a

---

* Prayer of St. Ignatius, http://www.loyolapress.com/suscipe-prayer-saint-ignatius-of-loyola. htm.

long way off, as they made their way along the Kidron Valley below. Jesus saw them coming. He could have simply walked over the crest of the Mount of Olives and disappeared into the Judean wilderness.

To tell the truth, he "saw them coming" weeks before that and could have eluded them at any time.

But his burning desire to save us was greater than his natural aversion to torture. His love was even stronger than death. "Unless a grain of wheat falls into the earth and dies, it remains alone; but if it dies, it bears much fruit" (John 12:24). Jesus knew that his death would be fruitful beyond all imagining. And being fruitful was more important to him than being safe or comfortable.

We gratefully celebrate this love in every Eucharist, remembering it most solemnly during Holy Week.

However, the Lord calls us not just to remember it, but to imitate it. We are called to be not just believers, but disciples. Jesus lost his natural human life, but he was given in return a new, risen humanity, which explodes the limits of the humanity we know.

We all have a life to which we're rather attached; people, places, things, and activities with which we are comfortable. My life may not be perfect, but it's familiar. And it's mine. In Lent, the Lord invites me not just to give up dessert for a few weeks, but to give up myself. He asks me to die to my own plans, my own will, and put my destiny entirely in his hands. Incidentally, that is what baptism is supposed to mean—that "it is no longer I who live, but Christ who lives in me" (Galatians 2:20). It means that I'm no longer in the driver's seat, but I've put Jesus there. That all that is dearest to me, I've put on the altar, and I will only take it back if the Lord gives it back.

Why would we do such a radical thing? Only if we truly believe that planting the seed of our lives and dreams in the fertile soil of the Lord's vineyard will produce much fruit. That we, like the apostles, will grow to be more than we'd ever hoped we'd be. That he would do through us, as through them, more than we'd ever dreamed possible.

So here's the final question: Is being fruitful more important to you than being safe…or comfortable…or in control?

DAY 38

Holy Thursday is not a holy day of obligation. But plan to go to the Mass of the Lord's Supper. If possible remain afterward for at least an hour of Adoration, staying awake with Jesus on the night that the disciples left him alone with his anguish in the garden. Whether in Church during Adoration or at home, read John 13—17, the Last Supper discourse of our Lord.

On Holy Thursday, the night before he died, the Lord Jesus made some startling changes in the ritual of the Passover meal. Instead of being content with the traditional Jewish table blessing over the bread, Jesus proclaimed, "Take, eat; this is my body" (Matthew 26:26). Over the third cup of wine, known as the cup of blessing, he said, "Drink of it, all of you, for this is my blood" (Matthew 26:27–28). Then he commanded the disciples, "Do this in memory of me" (Luke 22:19).

Obedient to the wishes of the Savior, we remember and reenact this solemn moment in a special way each Holy Thursday, but more frequently in every Mass. Indeed, the Catholic Church teaches that in the Eucharist the Communion wafer and the altar wine are transformed and really become the body and blood of Jesus Christ. Have you ever met anyone who has found this Catholic doctrine to be a bit hard to take?

If so, you shouldn't be surprised. When Jesus spoke about eating his flesh and drinking his blood in John 6, his words met with less than an enthusiastic reception. "How can this man give us his flesh to eat? This is a hard saying; who can listen to it?" (John 6:52, 60). In fact, so many of his disciples abandoned him over this that Jesus had to ask the twelve if they also planned to quit. It's interesting that Jesus did not run after his disciples, saying, "Don't go—I was just speaking metaphorically!"

How did the early Church interpret these challenging words of Jesus? Here's an interesting fact. One charge the pagan Romans lodged against the Christians was cannibalism. Why? You guessed it: They heard that this sect regularly met to eat and drink human flesh and blood. Did the early

Christians say, "Wait a minute—it's only a symbol"? Not at all. When trying to explain the Eucharist to the Roman Emperor around A.D. 155, St. Justin did not mince words: "For we do not receive these things as common bread or common drink; but as Jesus Christ our Saviour being incarnate by God's Word took flesh and blood for our salvation, so also we have been taught that the food consecrated by the word of prayer which comes from him…is the flesh and blood of that incarnate Jesus."*

Not many Christians questioned the real presence of Christ's body and blood in the Eucharist until the Middle Ages. In trying to explain how bread and wine are changed into the body and blood of Christ, several theologians went astray and needed to be corrected by Church authority. Then St. Thomas Aquinas came along and offered an explanation that became classic. In our everyday experience of life, he taught, appearances change, but deep down, the essence of a thing stays the same. For example, if, in a fit of midlife crisis, I trade my minivan for a Ferrari, abandon my wife and five kids to be a tanned, bleached-blond beach bum, buff up at the gym, and take a trip to the plastic surgeon, I'd look a lot different on the surface. But for all my trouble, deep down I'd still substantially be the same person as when I started.

St. Thomas said the Eucharist is the one instance of change we encounter in this world that is exactly the opposite. The appearances of bread and wine stay the same, but the very essence (or substance) of these realities, which can't be viewed by a microscope, is totally transformed. What was once bread and wine is now Christ's Body and Blood. A handy word was coined to describe this unique change. Transformation of the *sub-stance* ("what stands-under the surface"), came to be called *transubstantiation*.

What makes this happen? The power of God's Spirit and Word. After praying for the Spirit to come (*epiclesis*), the priest, who stands in the place of Christ, repeats the words of the God-man: "This is my Body; this is my Blood." Sounds to me like Genesis 1: The mighty wind (read "Spirit") whips over the surface of the water, and God's Word resounds with "Let there be

---

* From the translation of the First Apology of Justin found in Cyril Richardson, *Early Christian Fathers*. (New York: Touchstone, 1995), I Apol 66, p. 286.

light" and there was light. It is no harder to believe in the Eucharist than to believe in creation.

But why did Jesus arrange for this transformation of bread and wine? Because he intended another kind of transformation. The bread and wine are transformed into the Body and Blood of Christ, which are, in turn, meant to transform us. The Lord desires us to be transformed from a motley crew of imperfect individuals into the Body of Christ, come to full stature.

Our evangelical brethren speak often of an intimate, personal relationship with Jesus. But I ask you, how much more personal and intimate can you get? We receive the Lord's body into our physical body so that we may become him whom we receive!

It is this astounding gift that we remember and celebrate every Holy Thursday.

DAY 39

On Good Friday, free up some time, preferably from noon to 3 P.M., as a media-free zone of silence and prayer. Follow the prayer suggestions for Good Friday in the appendix of this book.

Terrorism is nothing new. It's probably as old as the human race.

In fact, the cradle of civilization, now known as Iraq, was the home of the most infamous terrorists of antiquity, the Assyrians. Their goal was to conquer their neighbors in a way that would minimize initial resistance and subsequent rebellion. To do this, they knew fear would be their greatest weapon. The simple threat of death for those who resisted was not enough, because many would prefer death to slavery. So the Assyrians developed the technology to produce the maximum amount of pain for the longest amount of time prior to death. It was called crucifixion. This ingenious procedure proved to be a very effective terror tactic indeed.

It was the policy of the Roman Empire to adopt from conquered peoples whatever appeared useful. They found crucifixion an excellent tool of intimidation. The humiliation of being stripped naked to die in a public spectacle was particularly loathsome to Jews, for whom public nudity was an abomination. Incidentally, crucifixion was deemed so horrible that Roman law forbade it to be carried out on a Roman citizen, even a traitor. It was reserved only for slaves and conquered peoples.

Non-Christians have often asked a very good question: Why do Christians adorn their churches, homes, and necks with a symbol of abasement, terror, and torture? Why build an entire religion around the cross?

In the twelfth century, St. Anselm explained it this way. Our first parent's sin was all about pride, disobedience, and self-love. Deceived by the serpent, Adam and Eve ate the forbidden fruit in defiance of God because they wanted to exalt themselves as his equal. The results were catastrophic—loss of communion with God, each other, and the created universe. The history of the human race has been a story in which each one of us, weakened by the impact of this sin on our nature, have followed its pattern, proudly refusing to obey God and love our neighbor.

Anselm pointed out that sin constitutes an infinite offense against the goodness and honor of God. Having been created free and responsible, bound by the law of justice, our race is obliged to offer acts of love, humility, and obedience to God that are powerful enough both to cancel out the long legacy of disobedience, pride, and selfishness and to restore our friendship with him.

The problem is, our wounded race could not begin to attempt such a task. So the Father sent his Eternal Word to become man and accomplish the task in our place, to substitute for us. For the immortal, infinite God to empty himself and unite himself to a limited, vulnerable human nature was already a feat of unimaginable love and humility. But for redemption to be complete, the hero would have to withstand the greatest fury that hell and fallen humanity could hurl against him: the cross.

Surely after the crowds he had healed and fed cried, "Crucify him!" and his own apostles fled, Jesus would realize it wasn't worth it. Surely he would curse the ingrates and use his divine power to free himself as many suggested in their taunts. But no. His was love to the end (see John 13:1). His death was the clear and undeniable manifestation of the triumph of obedience over disobedience, love over selfishness, humility over pride.

Good Friday was the D-Day of the human race. Since Pentecost, the power of Christ's obedient, humble, unstoppable love has been made available to all who are willing to share it, producing martyrs and saints in every generation, down to the Maximilian Kolbes and Mother Teresas of our own era.

So the cross is not only victorious, it is fruitful. It bore the fruit of salvation in the loving act of Christ but has kept bearing new fruit throughout the ages. That's why, if you go to the Church of San Clemente in Rome, you'll see one of the most stunning mosaics in the Eternal City: the ancient instrument of subjection and death wrapped with verdant vines supporting fruit of every shape and size—the triumphant cross become the tree of life.

DAY 40

Go to the Easter Vigil (even if you are going to Mass again on Easter) in order to intercede for and celebrate with those being received into full communion with the Church. And if you can't go, renew your baptismal vows on your own and meditate on the magnificent Easter proclamation known as the Exsultet.

The ancient world was thickly populated with gods. Those open-minded Romans actually collected as many as they could find and enshrined them all in a special building that still stands today: the Pantheon (meaning "all gods" in Greek).

The Israelites ran into quite a few of these idols. There were the animal gods of the Egyptians. Then there were the fertility gods of the Canaanites, worshiped through ritual prostitution. There was Moloch, the god of the Ammonites, who demanded the sacrifice of infant children. Joshua 24 is all about the Israelites making a conscious decision to serve the Lord, the God of Abraham, Isaac, and Jacob, instead of these idols. After all, they knew you had to serve one god or another.

We, unfortunately, are not wise enough to know this. Many of us in the twenty-first century think we are autonomous and able to run our own lives, thank you very much. But the abortion holocaust proves that the spirit of Moloch is alive and well on planet earth. And while fertility is not in style, one look at our entertainment industry shows us that sex makes the world go round.

So a conscious decision is required, but this decision is not a one-time deal. It has to be renewed again and again. The Israelites said yes to Yahweh's proposal in Exodus 19 and accepted the wedding band of the Ten Commandments. But forty years later, facing new challenges and new idols, they had to recommit themselves at Shechem.

Really, the relationship between us (the Church) and Christ is a lot like a marriage. That's what Ephesians 5 is about. This union is intimate. Christ binds himself to care lovingly for us as for his own body, nourishing us with Word and Eucharist, cleansing us in baptism and penance. For our part, we submit to his direction, trusting in his love. He's not just our Savior; he's our Lord. We obey and serve him. This is a permanent, lasting relationship. Therefore it has to be renewed on a daily basis.

All of the many disciples who followed Jesus around Galilee once made a decision to follow Jesus. But when faced with Jesus's hard teaching on the Eucharist (see John 6), it was just too much for many of them. They hadn't bargained for this. They were quintessential "heretics." The word *heresy* means "choice"—picking and choosing only those doctrines that fit into one's comfort zone and don't threaten one's idols.

In the early centuries of the Church, the nature of true discipleship was manifested dramatically in the baptismal ceremony. On Holy Saturday night the catechumens would gather in the baptistery. The first thing they would do is face west, the place where darkness swallows up the sun each night, and repudiate Satan, their old master. After this divorce decree, they turned to the East, the direction of the rising sun, and professed their vows to be faithful to their new, triune spouse. After passing through the water, they were led into the church, draped in white robes and holding candles in what St. Cyril called a nuptial procession. There, after confirmation, they enjoyed the wedding feast of the Eucharist. Every Sunday thereafter they remembered their baptism as they once again partook of the wedding feast. And every day they were encouraged to renew their vows by repeating the sign that was first traced on their foreheads on that special day—the sign of the cross, their wedding band.

C.S. Lewis once wrote a fantasy that I highly recommend called *The Great Divorce*. Our greatest temptation is the illusion that we can have peaceful coexistence in our lives between good and evil, between God and idols. The reality is that they are mutually exclusive. If we compromise and try to serve both, our life will be a chaotic battleground, and we'll be the casualties.

> Exult, let them exult, the hosts of heaven,
> exult, let Angel ministers of God exult,
> let the trumpet of salvation

sound aloud our mighty King's triumph!
Be glad, let earth be glad, as glory floods her,
ablaze with light from her eternal King,
let all corners of the earth be glad,
knowing an end to gloom and darkness.
Rejoice, let Mother Church also rejoice,
arrayed with the lightning of his glory,
let this holy building shake with joy,
filled with the mighty voices of the peoples.
(Therefore, dearest friends,
standing in the awesome glory of this holy light,
invoke with me, I ask you,
the mercy of God almighty,
that he, who has been pleased to number me,
though unworthy, among the Levites,
may pour into me his light unshadowed,
that I may sing this candle's perfect praises).
(*Deacon:* The Lord be with you.
People: And with your spirit.)
Deacon: Lift up your hearts.
People: We lift them up to the Lord.
Deacon: Let us give thanks to the Lord our God.
People: It is right and just.

It is truly right and just,
with ardent love of mind and heart
and with devoted service of our voice,
to acclaim our God invisible, the almighty Father,
and Jesus Christ, our Lord, his Son, his Only Begotten.

Who for our sake paid Adam's debt to the eternal Father,
and, pouring out his own dear Blood,
wiped clean the record of our ancient sinfulness.

These, then, are the feasts of Passover,

in which is slain the Lamb, the one true Lamb,

whose Blood anoints the doorposts of believers.

This is the night,

when once you led our forebears, Israel's children,

from slavery in Egypt

and made them pass dry-shod through the Red Sea.

This is the night

that with a pillar of fire

banished the darkness of sin.

This is the night

that even now throughout the world,

sets Christian believers apart from worldly vices

and from the gloom of sin,

leading them to grace

and joining them to his holy ones.

This is the night

when Christ broke the prison-bars of death

and rose victorious from the underworld.

Our birth would have been no gain,

had we not been redeemed.

O wonder of your humble care for us!

O love, O charity beyond all telling,

to ransom a slave you gave away your Son!

O truly necessary sin of Adam,

destroyed completely by the Death of Christ!

O happy fault

that earned for us so great, so glorious a Redeemer!

O truly blessed night,
worthy alone to know the time and hour
when Christ rose from the underworld!

This is the night
of which it is written:
The night shall be as bright as day,
dazzling is the night for me,
and full of gladness.

The sanctifying power of this night
dispels wickedness, washes faults away,
restores innocence to the fallen, and joy to mourners,
drives out hatred, fosters concord, and brings down the mighty.

On this, your night of grace, O holy Father,
accept this candle, a solemn offering,
the work of bees and of your servants' hands,
an evening sacrifice of praise,
this gift from your most holy Church.

But now we know the praises of this pillar,
which glowing fire ignites for God's honor,
a fire into many flames divided,
yet never dimmed by sharing of its light,
for it is fed by melting wax,
drawn out by mother bees
to build a torch so precious.

O truly blessed night,
when things of heaven are wed to those of earth,
and divine to the human.

Therefore, O Lord,
we pray you that this candle,

hallowed to the honor of your name,
may persevere undimmed,
to overcome the darkness of this night.
Receive it as a pleasing fragrance,
and let it mingle with the lights of heaven.
May this flame be found still burning
by the Morning Star:
the one Morning Star who never sets,
Christ your Son,
who, coming back from death's domain,
has shed his peaceful light on humanity,
and lives and reigns for ever and ever.
Amen.

EASTER SUNDAY

The serpent's bite was a deadly one. The venom had worked its way deep into the heart of the entire human race, doing its gruesome work. The antivenin was unavailable until Christ appeared. One drop was all that was needed, so potent was this antidote. Yet it was not like him to be stingy. He poured out all he had, down to the last drop. The sacrifice of his entire life, poured out at the foot of the cross—this was the Son's answer to the problem of sin.

Three days later came the Father's answer to the problem of death. It was equally extravagant. Jesus was not simply brought back to life, like Lazarus. That would have been resuscitation, the mere return to normal, human life, with all its limitations, including death. Lazarus ultimately had to go through it all again—the suffering, the dying, the grieving family, the burial. Jesus did not "come back." He passed over, passed through. His resurrection meant that he would no longer be subject to suffering, death, and decay. Death, as St. Paul said, would have no more power over him.

You may say that physical death was not the worst consequence of sin, and you'd be right. Separation from God—spiritual death—is indeed much more fearsome. But enough with the talk that physical death is "beautiful" and "natural." It is not. Our bodies are not motor vehicles driven around by our souls. We do not junk them when they wear out and then buy other ones (by the way, that's one problem with the idea of reincarnation). No, our bodies are an essential dimension of who we are. Our bodies and immortal souls are intimately and completely intertwined, which makes us so different from both angels and animals. Therefore, death separates what God has joined. It is, then, entirely natural that we rebel against it and shudder before it. Remember, even the God-Man trembled in the Garden of Gethsemane.

Jesus confronts death head on, for our sake. The Roman Easter sequence, a traditional poem/song stretching back into the days of the early Church, highlights the drama: "*Mors et vita duello, conflixere mirando; dux vitae mortuus regnat vivus*" ("Death and life dueled in a marvelous conflict; the Dead Ruler of Life reigns Alive!"). Recall that *Lord of the Rings* character Gandalf the Grey, who sacrificed himself to take out the demonic Balrog, returns as Gandalf the White. The devout Catholic writer J.R.R. Tolkien heard the sequence sung for many Easters before he wrote his famous trilogy.

"He descended into hell," says the Apostles' Creed, meaning that Jesus endured the wrenching apart of body and soul for our sakes and came out the other side endowed with a new, different, glorified humanity. How does the Bible describe it? Well, Mary Magdalene did not recognize the Risen Christ at first, until he called her by name. The disciples on the road to Emmaus didn't recognize him either, even after walking with him for several miles. But, on the other hand, doubting Thomas shows us that Christ's wounds were still evident. And though he could pass through locked doors, he proved he was not a ghost by asking for something to eat. In 1 Corinthians 15, St. Paul describes Jesus's risen body as a "spiritual body," which might sound like an oxymoron. But we have to take off our shoes here and realize we are on holy ground—there are no words adequate to describe the awesome reality of the new humanity he won for us.

Resurrection is not something that Christ intended to keep for himself. All that Jesus has he shares with us: his Father, Mother, Spirit, body, blood, soul, and divinity, and even his risen life. And we can begin to share in this life now, experiencing its regenerating, transforming power in our souls and even in our bodies. We have access to it in many wonderful ways, but most especially in the Eucharist. For the body of Christ that we receive in the host is his risen, glorified body, given to us so that we too might live forever (see John 6:40–65).

Each of us will have to pass through physical death. But we will not do so alone. Jesus will be with us, just as the Father was with him as he made his perilous passage. And while we will experience indescribable joy when our souls "see" him face-to-face, this is not the end of the story. He will return. And when he does, his resurrection will have its final and ultimate impact. Joy will be increased still further when he makes our bodies like his own, in glory. "I look forward to the resurrection of the dead, and the life of the world to come. Amen!"

CELEBRATING THE EASTER SEASON

"We don't display the cross with Christ still hanging from it like you Catholics do," boasted a neighbor of a friend of mine. "We are Easter people. We focus on his resurrection."

The fact that Catholics revere the crucifix doesn't mean that we don't believe that Jesus rose from the dead. But I have to admit that the way Catholics observe Lent versus the way we celebrate Easter often feeds into this misconception.

Catholic parishes are packed on Ash Wednesday. Even the ranks of those who attend daily Mass swell during Lent. There are Stations of the Cross, Lenten missions, parish fish fries—forty days of spiritual exercises, penance, and focus on Jesus's suffering.

Then Easter rolls around. Whether it is the Easter Vigil, a sunrise service, or a regular Sunday Mass, the liturgy is magnificent. Lilies, bonnets, chocolates, and bunnies appear, and families feast together to celebrate the occasion. But the next day, churches are virtually empty and everyone returns to business as usual.

This is not the way things went in the early Church! Easter, from at least the early fourth century, went for fifty days—from Easter Sunday through Pentecost. The first ecumenical Council of Nicaea in 325, the one that gave us the Nicene Creed, issued a decree that is still observed in Byzantine Catholic and Orthodox Churches. As a sign of rejoicing, the council prohibited kneeling during the liturgy until the end of the Pentecost celebration.

I don't advise that everyone abandon kneeling during Eastertide, since, for Catholics of the Latin or Roman rite, kneeling is a sign of adoration as well as penance. But we do need to recover the richness of Easter as an entire season of celebration.

The atheist philosopher Friedrich Nietzsche is quoted as saying, "If you Christians want me to believe in your redeemer, you need to look more redeemed!"*

The recovery of prolonged Easter joy is one of the keys not only to our own happiness, but to the new evangelization!

First, the concept of the Easter Octave needs to be recovered. In the book of Exodus, God commanded the Israelites to celebrate the greater feasts, such as Passover, for eight continuous days; a solemn assembly was to be held on the first and eighth days. So, liturgically, we celebrate Easter at highest pitch from Easter Sunday to Divine Mercy Sunday. Every day of this octave is considered a solemn feast in the Roman calendar. As such, if there is ever a time to go to daily Mass, the Easter Octave is it!

The choir leader's contract may not include leading music at all Easter Octave liturgies, but perhaps someone else could lead the congregation in singing the acclamations along with a few songs to make even an early morning Mass share in the festive spirit of the week.

Can't make it to daily Mass during the Octave? Read the Mass readings alone, or even better, with your spouse, roommate, or family. Don't have a missal? You can find the daily Mass readings online or by using smartphone apps such as Laudate or iMissal.

In my family, before we say grace, we employ the Easter greeting used in the Eastern Churches. I say, "Christ is risen!" The family responds, "He is risen indeed!"

We also discovered the beautiful Marian prayer specific to the Easter season, *Regina Caeli* (Queen of Heaven, Rejoice, Alleluia!). We learned it in both English and Latin, and we recite or sing it together before bed each night of Eastertide.

---

* Quoted in Celebrating Easter," www.crossroadsinitiative.com.

Regina Caeli (Queen of Heaven)

V. Queen of Heaven, rejoice, alleluia.

R. For He whom you did merit to bear, alleluia.

V. Has risen, as he said, alleluia.

R. Pray for us to God, alleluia.

V. Rejoice and be glad, O Virgin Mary, alleluia.

R. For the Lord has truly risen, alleluia.

Let us pray. O God, who gave joy to the world through the resurrection of Thy Son, our Lord Jesus Christ, grant we beseech Thee, that through the intercession of the Virgin Mary, His Mother, we may obtain the joys of everlasting life. Through the same Christ our Lord. Amen.

POST-LENTEN POSTSCRIPT

Increasing numbers of people are accepting fitness challenges sponsored by the local gym. They range from thirty, sixty, or ninety days, and at the end, we see before and after pictures of all the people who look so much better and happier after losing weight and toning up. The last thing they'd want is to return to the way they used to be. And most don't. They usually fight hard to protect their new state of vitality by maintaining the diet and workout routines that got them to where they are.

If you accepted the forty-day challenge presented in this book, you've had a spiritual makeover. It would make no sense to simply stop the spiritual exercises that you practiced during Lent once Easter arrives—instead, make them a permanent feature of your life! Then, next Lent, take out this book and let the Spirit guide you to incorporate still more of these training tips into your regimen. The call to holiness is the ultimate challenge, and there's no limit to how far you can go!

LENTEN RESOURCES

I've restricted the following list to give you some of the best resources I know, many of which my family and I personally have used. I've tried to limit myself mostly to books that are also available as audiobooks, either on CDs or as digital downloads you can listen to on a computer, iPod, or smartphone. Many of these resources and more are available on my website, dritaly.com, and new resources are continually being added there. Others can be found from a variety of vendors through an Internet search.

THE SCRIPTURAL ROSARY

Available either in a small hardcover booklet or on audio CD, this resource from the Christianica Center really helps make the rosary the meditative, contemplative prayer it is meant to be. A short Scripture verse between each Hail Mary keeps your mind on the mysteries. Both book and audio versions—which include the luminous as well as the joyful, sorrowful, and glorious mysteries—are available on dritaly.com.

BIBLE STUDY TOOLS

If you've never done an overview of the entire Bible from Genesis to Revelation, that is the place to start. The best tool for this is the Great Adventure Bible Timeline by Jeff Cavins. It is available at dritaly.com in either an eight-session or twenty-four-session format, on video or audio with workbooks. After that, more in-depth studies of particular books of the Bible are available from Great Adventure (dritaly.com) or Catholic Scripture Study International (cssprogram.net).

DVD VIDEOS FOR INSPIRATION: NONFICTION
(see dritaly.com and ignatius.com)

Jesus of Nazareth, directed by Franco Zeffirelli. This three part series of two-hour videos starts with the angel Gabriel's visit to Mary and concludes with the resurrection. In my opinion, it is the best video presentation of the whole life of Christ ever made.

A Man for All Seasons. Thomas Bolt wrote a marvelous play by this name on St. Thomas More and his confrontation with Henry VIII. Two movie versions of this were produced, the first starring Paul Scofield as Thomas, the second starring Charlton Heston. They are both superb.

The Scarlet and the Black, starring Gregory Peck. The true story of an Irish priest living at the Vatican in World War II and the amazing network he organized to hide Jews and escaped allied prisoners from the Gestapo.

Restless Heart: The Confessions of St. Augustine Extremely well-done drama of the life of one of the most passionate and colorful of the early Church fathers. *The Passion of the Christ*, directed by Mel Gibson. This is clearly inspiration, not entertainment. The violence is not gratuitous, but it reflects the reality of Christ's passion. Incredibly moving.

Becket. An older film about an advisor to the King of England who, after becoming Archbishop of Canterbury, defends the rights of the Church against his erstwhile friend and pays the price.

LIVES OF THE SAINTS

Joan of Arc, by Mark Twain. Few know that Twain considered his historical novel on Joan to be his most important work. He spent ten years researching it in France and truly captures her sanctity and beauty in a way that only Mark Twain can.

Something Beautiful for God, by Malcom Muggeridge. A very readable and engaging biography of Mother Teresa of Calcutta.

When the Church Was Young: The Voices of the Early Fathers, by Marcellino D'Ambrosio. The lives and teaching of the important figures from the first centuries of the Church, most of them saints and many of them martyrs.

Witness to Hope: The Biography of John Paul II, by George Weigel.

Pope John XXIII: A Spiritual Biography, by Christian Feldman.

The Autobiography of St. Therese of Lisieux. This book by the saint known as the Little Flower is an absolute gem.

Francis: The Journey and the Dream, by Murray Bodo. A life of St. Francis of Assisi.

Tortured for Christ, by Richard Wurmbrand. The story of Christian martyrs in Communist Romania told by a Lutheran pastor who was imprisoned and tortured for years.

The Guide to the Passion: 100 Questions about The Passion of the Christ, by Mark Shea, Tom Allen, Marcellino D'Ambrosio, Paul Thigpen, and Matt Pinto. Written to explain Mel Gibson's film, this little book goes much further; it explains the purpose, meaning, and nature of Christ's suffering.

BOOKS FOR ENTERTAINMENT AND INSPIRATION:
FICTION (WIDELY AVAILABLE)

Jesus used fictional tales called parables to teach spiritual truths. Many works of fiction, whether books or movies, can instruct and inspire even as they entertain. Film versions of some of these exist and are good—in most cases, the books are much better (audiobooks for these are also available). Here is a list of a few of my favorites.

The Chronicles of Narnia by C.S. Lewis. Yes, these were written for children, but I first read them as an adult, and now I reread them every few years. Amazing illustrations in fiction of the truths of faith and morality with dramatic portrayals of virtues and vices.

The Space Trilogy: Out of the Silent Planet, Perelandra, That Hideous Strength, by C.S. Lewis. Lesser known fiction by Lewis but profoundly enlightening and inspiring.

The Great Divorce, by C.S. Lewis. A little over a hundred pages, this is readable even by those with limited time. It is a fantasy that provides more insight into heaven, hell, good and evil, vice and virtue than most theology books on the subject.

The Screwtape Letters, by C.S. Lewis. Another short fictional book of Lewis that consists of a senior demon writing letters of instruction to a junior demon on the strategy of temptation. Humorous but highly enlightening.

The Hobbit and *The Lord of the Rings* by J.R.R. Tolkein. Less obvious than C.S. Lewis, Tolkein is no less Christian in his message.

Mini-Retreat for Good Friday and the Triduum

Sundown on Holy Thursday marks the beginning of three sacred days (Triduum) that changed the destiny of the human race. Few of us have sufficient time to make use of all the following prayer suggestions during these holy days, but it would be a tragedy to let this season of grace go by without taking some time for extended prayer and reflection. So steal away for as much time as you can and let the Spirit help you pick and choose which devotions will best help you make the most of this special time.

HOLY THURSDAY

John 13:1—18:27 deals with the words and deeds of Jesus on the evening of Holy Thursday, including the washing the feet of the disciples, the Last Supper discourse and priestly prayer of our Lord, Jesus's arrest in the Garden of Gethsemane, and Peter's denial. Prayerfully read as much of this as you can—these are some of the most powerful and moving chapters in the entire Bible.

GOOD FRIDAY MORNING

1. Repentance for Complicity in Christ's Betrayal (approximately sixty minutes)

Read Luke 22:39—23:26, but first ask the Holy Spirit to help you answer these questions in the course of your reading:

- In what way am I an accomplice in the betrayal and execution of the Lord?
- Whom in the Gospel narrative do I most resemble: The disciples asleep in the garden? The cowardly Peter? The irresponsible Pilate? Someone else? Write down the answers in your journal, if you keep one.

In response to the Spirit's prompting:

- Pray a prayer repenting of the particular sins in your life that have made you an accomplice in the Lord's betrayal and execution.

- Confidently ask the Lord to help you to uproot these sins from your life.
- Finally, seal this process by a slow, prayerful reading of Psalm 51. You might even feel led to memorize a portion of it.

2. Putting on the Mind of Christ (approximately thirty minutes)

Now that we have cast off the "mind" of darkness, we can put on "the mind of Christ."

- Read Philippians 2:5–11 and consider how Jesus's humble self-offering on the cross was the perfect manifestation of his "mind."
- Read Philippians 2:14–15 and see how St. Paul commands us to have the same mind as the Lord.
- Ask the Lord what particular characteristics of his mind he wishes to impart to you in a new way during these special days: Humility? Obedience? A new degree of service or love? Some other characteristic? Ask him to show you how this is to be worked out concretely and practically in the present circumstances of your life. Write in your journal whatever the Lord tells you.
- Say yes to what he wants to do in you and ask him to make it happen by the power of his Spirit.
- Use Psalm 116, one of the "Hallel" psalms prayed by Jesus at the Last Supper, to express your gratitude to the Lord for freeing you from sin through his death and for bestowing upon you his mind.

GOOD FRIDAY AFTERNOON

The most solemn time of the whole Christian year is from noon to 3 P.M. on Good Friday since that was the time of the Lord's agony on the cross according to the Gospel of John. During this time, we should strive to honor the death of the Lord in the most personal and heartfelt way possible.

- Meditate slowly and deeply upon Isaiah 52:13—53:13. This is the song of the Suffering Servant.
- Read Zechariah 12:10 and respond with a silent prayer of mourning and adoration. You may want to make use of "the Jesus Prayer" which consists

of the following petition repeated over and over: "Lord Jesus Christ, Son of the living God, have mercy on me, a sinner."

- In Jesus's time, the way to refer to a psalm was not by its number but by its first line. Jesus's cry from the cross, "My God, my God, why have you forsaken me," is the first line of Psalm 22. Read this entire psalm slowly, as if the whole thing were Jesus's prayer from the cross.

- Meditate on Hebrews 9:11–28. This Scripture relates how Christ the High Priest, by the shedding of his own blood, entered the sanctuary once and for all.

- Read the selections from Melito of Sardis and Ephrem below. Use the thanksgiving prayer that follows to help you express gratitude for what the Lord did for us through his suffering and death.

> Our Lord subjected his might, and they seized him,
> so that through his living death he might give life to Adam.
> He gave his hands to be pierced by nails
> to make up for the hand which plucked the fruit.
> He was struck on his cheek in the judgment room
> to make up for the mouth that ate in Eden.
> And while Adam's foot was free, his feet were pierced.
> Our Lord was stripped that we might be clothed.
> With the gall and vinegar he sweetened
> the poison of the serpent which had bitten men.*

> This is the one who patiently endured many things in many people:
> This is the one who was murdered in Abel, and bound as a sacrifice in Isaac,
> and exiled in Jacob, and sold in Joseph,
> and exposed in Moses, and sacrificed in the lamb,
> and hunted down in David, and dishonored in the prophets.
> This is the one who became human in a virgin,

---

* St. Ephrem (fourth-century Church Father), (Sermo de Domino Nostro, 3–4, 9: Opera edit. Lamy, 1, 152–158, 166–168).

who was hanged on the tree, who was buried in the earth,

who was resurrected from among the dead,

and who raised mankind up out of the grave below to the heights of heaven.

The one who hung the earth in space, is himself hanged;

the one who fixed the heavens in place, is himself impaled;

the one who firmly fixed all things, is himself firmly fixed to the tree.

The Lord is insulted, God has been murdered,

the King of Israel has been destroyed by the right hand of Israel.

This is the lamb that was slain. This is the lamb that was silent.

This is the one who was taken from the flock, and was dragged to sacrifice,

and was killed in the evening, and was buried at night;

the one who was not broken while on the tree,

who did not see dissolution while in the earth.

who rose up from the dead, and who raised up mankind from the grave below.*

Thanksgiving Prayers for Use During Holy Week

Father of Mercy and Salvation,

As you planted the tree of life in the Garden of Eden, so you have planted the cross of your Son in the New Paradise, replacing the tree that brought us death with the gracious tree that brings us life.

Response: Glory to you, O Lord.

As you judged the earth by water and saved Noah by means of the ark, so you judged the world in the water of your Son's pierced side, and saved a remnant through the wood of his cross.

Response: Glory to you, O Lord.

As Abraham's only son, the son he loved, bore to Moriah the wood of his sacrifice, so your only Son, the beloved Son, bore his cross

---

* St. Melito of Sardis (second-century Church Father), "On the Passover" (Mp/ 65–71; SC 123, 95–101).

to Golgotha, that the blessing of Abraham might be given to the world.

Response: Glory to you, O Lord.

As Joseph was sold by his brothers and reckoned as dead, yet was raised in glory to the King's right hand, so you Son was delivered to death by his brothers and raised in glory by your Spirit to rule at your side.

Response: Glory to you, O Lord.

As the blood of the lamb turned away the angel of death and delivered Israel from Pharaoh's reign, so the blood of your Son has saved us from death and delivered us from bondage to Satan and the world.

Response: Glory to you, O Lord.

As the High Priest entered the Holy of Holies with blood to atone for the sins of the people, so your Son entered the true Holy Place and presented the blood that atones for the sins of the world.

Response: Glory to you, O Lord.

As Moses raised the serpent in the wilderness to heal those who suffered for their sin, so the Son of Man was lifted up on the cross to bear our sin and make us whole.

Response: Glory to you, O Lord.

As Jonah lay three days in the belly of the whale, and was raised from death to preach repentance to the Gentiles, so your Son was raised from the bowels of the earth to reconcile all nations to yourself.

Response: Glory to you, O Lord.

HOLY SATURDAY

Today is a day of waiting, a day of silence. Most Christian churches allow no celebrations on this day, including burials, weddings, the Eucharist or the Lord's Supper. In some churches, Communion is only offered to those in imminent danger of death. All this is a tremendous reminder of salvation by grace working through faith. Our Christian life is completely dependent upon the Lord's resurrection, but there is absolutely nothing we can do to make this happen. So we wait and meditate on the statement of the Apostles' Creed: "He descended into hell."

- Ponder Psalm 16 and Psalm 24. The "gates" mentioned in the latter psalm can refer to the gates of hell, which Jesus, the man with clean hands and pure heart, enters after his righteous death in order to liberate those who are held captive there.
- Meditate on Romans 6:3–11.
- Read the amazing Holy Saturday homily preserved from the days of the early Church below.

> It is he who was made man of the Virgin, he who was hung on the tree; it is he who was buried in the earth, raised from the dead, and taken up to the heights of heaven. He is the mute lamb, the slain lamb, the lamb born of Mary, the fair ewe. He was seized from the flock, dragged off to be slaughtered, sacrificed in the evening, and buried at night. On the tree no bone of his was broken; in the earth his body knew no decay He is the One who rose from the dead, and who raised man from the depths of the tomb. Something strange is happening—there is a great silence on earth today, a great silence and stillness. The whole earth keeps silence because the King is asleep. The earth trembled and is still because God has fallen asleep in the flesh and he has raised up all who have slept ever since the world began. God has died in the flesh and hell trembles with fear.
>
> He has gone to search for our first parent, as for a lost sheep. Greatly desiring to visit those who live in darkness and in the shadow of death, he has gone to free from sorrow the captives Adam and Eve, he who is both God and the son of Eve. The Lord approached them bearing the cross, the weapon that had won him the victory. At the sight of him Adam, the first man he had created, struck his breast in terror and cried out to everyone: "My Lord be with you all." Christ answered him: "And with your spirit." He took

him by the hand and raised him up, saying: "Awake, O sleeper, and rise from the dead, and Christ will give you light."

I am your God, who for your sake have become your son. Out of love for you and for your descendants I now by my own authority command all who are held in bondage to come forth, all who are in darkness to be enlightened, all who are sleeping to arise. I order you, O sleeper, to awake. I did not create you to be held a prisoner in hell. Rise from the dead, for I am the life of the dead. Rise up, work of my hands, you who were created in my image. Rise, let us leave this place, for you are in me and I am in you; together we form only one person and we cannot be separated. For your sake I, your God, became your son; I, the Lord, took the form of a slave; I, whose home is above the heavens, descended to the earth and beneath the earth. For your sake, for the sake of man, I became like a man without help, free among the dead. For the sake of you, who left a garden, I was betrayed to the Jews in a garden, and I was crucified in a garden.

See on my face the spittle I received in order to restore to you the life I once breathed into you. See there the marks of the blows I received in order to refashion your warped nature in my image. On my back see the marks of the scourging I endured to remove the burden of sin that weighs upon your back. See my hands, nailed firmly to a tree, for you who once wickedly stretched out your hand to a tree.

I slept on the cross and a sword pierced my side for you who slept in paradise and brought forth Eve from your side. My side has healed the pain in yours. My sleep will rouse you from your sleep in hell. The sword that pierced me has sheathed the sword that was turned against you.

Rise, let us leave this place. The enemy led you out of the earthly paradise. I will not restore you to that paradise, but I will enthrone you in heaven. I forbade you the tree that was only a symbol of life, but see, I who am life itself am now one with you. I appointed cherubim to guard you as slaves are guarded, but now I make them worship you as God. The throne formed by cherubim awaits you, its bearers swift and eager. The bridal chamber is adorned, the banquet is ready, the eternal dwelling places are prepared, the treasure houses of all good things lie open. The kingdom of heaven has been prepared for you from all eternity.*

EASTER WEEK

The resurrection of the Lord is too great of an event to celebrate for only one day! Following the Jewish practice of celebrating the Passover for eight days (an "octave"), the early Church celebrated Easter in high gear for an entire week. One great way for us to continue this tradition is to read a different resurrection Scripture each day of Easter week and attend Mass daily, or at least on as many days during the Easter octave as we can.

Monday—Matthew 28:8–15

Tuesday—John 20:11–18

Wednesday—Luke 24:13–35

Thursday—Luke 24:35–48

Friday—John 21:1–14

Saturday—Mark 16:9–15

Sunday—John 20:19–31

---

* From the Office of Readings for Holy Saturday, this homily is from an unknown fourth century Greek writer (PG 43, 439, 462ff).

ABOUT THE AUTHOR

Marcellino D'Ambrosio is a world-renowned commentator on religious issues. With a Ph.D. in theology (under Cardinal Avery Dulles), nine years of university teaching, and hundreds of published articles, Marcellino has a wealth of knowledge and knows how to make it accessible for a wide variety of audiences. Known as "Dr. Italy," he has a popular website, Facebook page, and Twitter feed and appears weekly on a variety of Catholic TV and radio networks. His books include *When the Church Was Young: Voices of the Early Church Fathers.*